The Memories That We Leave Behind

A POETRY BOOK
COLLECTION

Written by:
Ronald Black

Gotham Books

30 N Gould St.
Ste. 20820, Sheridan, WY 82801
https://gothambooksinc.com/

Phone: 1 (307) 464-7800

© 2023 *Ronald Black*. All rights reserved.

No part of this book may be reproduced, stored in a retrieval system, or transmitted by any means without the written permission of the author.

Published by Gotham Books (May 28, 2023)

ISBN: 979-8-88775-308-9 (P)
ISBN: 979-8-88775-309-6 (E)

Because of the dynamic nature of the Internet, any web addresses or links contained in this book may have changed since publication and may no longer be valid.

The views expressed in this work are solely those of the author and do not necessarily reflect the views of the publisher, and the publisher hereby disclaims any responsibility for them.

Introduction

Ronald Black ventures off into a few different forms and styles of poetry but seems most comfortable with varying kinds of stanzas. Some of the poems come complete with a long explanation when relevant at the end if more background information is helpful in understanding the motivation and message of a particular poem.

Readers of any age or background will be able to see themselves in some poems while broadening their horizons to a different perspective or way of life in others. Eye-opening and revealing, each piece offers the reader food for thought and a look through the author's eyes at the world around him.

Dedication

I dedicated this book to my loving wife Shirly Black and son Ronald Black Jr.

About the Author

The life that I have had to live has been very difficult but the love in my heart kept me strong even when I sometimes may have felt alone. I have cried my share of tears and I have suffered for many years but I have kept the love in my heart. We are human and we make mistakes but as long as we live there will always be another road for us to take.

Contents

The Memories That We Leave Behind 1
I Am Alive With The Joy That I Can
    See 2
A Legacy Of Love 3
Loved In Our Home............................... 4
Sometimes We Just Have To Slow
    Down.. 5
Adventures That Life Will Put Us
    Through... 6
Time Of Change Upon Us 7
Changes Of Minds Changes Of Hearts 8
Music In Me And Music In You........... 9
I Can Hear The Words That You Say 11
Words That We Wonder To Say........ 12
I Did It All For You 13
It Will Amaze The World 14
We Lost Someone The Other Day...... 15
The Clicking Of Our Hearts................ 16
Let Love Reach Deep Inside My Soul
    17
When A Time Of Change Comes Upon
    Us.. 18
To See Beyond The Veils Of Time ... 19
Looking On The Inside Of You 20
Imagine Yourself Being His Age 21
To Walk Along The Beach 22
Turnaround Faces Changing Places... 23
A Simple Thought Flows Through My
    Mind 24
The Things That You Did Wrong...... 25
When You Least Expect Something
    Happens 26
I Am Just A Child 28
Never Mind What Was Said Yesterday
    29
It Is Okay to Say Good-Bye................ 31
Here Is A Prayer From Me 32

It Is The Morning Of Another Day 33
Could You Ever Imagine The Face You
    Will See... 35
A Love Story Once Told 37
Your Temper's Too High................... 38
Come Go With Me To Another World
    39
Differences In The Lives That We Live
    40
You Know That I Have Always Been
    There For You 41
Another Year Has Come And Gone .. 42
You Are Not A Child Why Do You
    Cry? 43
You Heard Some Bad News................ 45
Little Child Come With Me 46
Turnaround Faces Changing Places... 48
Memories Of A Love That I Used To
    Feel 49
As The River Runs Fast Like The
    Memories Of The Past................. 50
Walking Down That Dusky Road...... 51
It Is Time To Wipe The Tears From
    Your Eyes 52
Will You Smile When You Hear 53
I Cannot Take The Things That You
    Are Doing To Me......................... 54
When You Are Looking At Me 55
You Became The Voice Of Everyone
    That Were Lost............................ 56
We Cannot Be Given Everything....... 57
Before The Moment Will Disappear . 58
I Live For The Hunt 59
As We Live Our Lives Year By Year 60
I Have Been With You For Such A
    Long Time   I've been with
    you for such a long time 61

Here Is To Me and Here Is To You ... 62
No More Tears Will I Cry 63
When Love Is More Than A Dream .. 65
Moving In Slow Motion 66
What Is It Going To Be 67
Maybe You Think Love Has Grown
   Strong 68
When Love May Not Be Real 69
A Promise Made To You 70
Watching You For Some Time 71
I Cannot Take The Things That You
   Are Doing To Me 72
I Can See Inside of You 73
Our Love Is Worth Defending 74
Can You Tell Me Why 75
There Will Come A Day 77
There is a sound that I Sometimes hear
   79
I Have Traveled Near And Far 80
I Wake Up To The Sound Of A Voice
   81
Remember Me 82
When Life Takes Us Down A Bumpy
   Road 84
Looking Up At The Mountaintop 85
What We Can And Cannot Achieve .. 86
Imagination And Me 87
The Flowers Of Our Lives Struggle To
   Survive 88
I Pray That It Is Not Too Late 89
When I Count To Three I know Where
   You Will Be 90
I Never Thought You Could Be
   Interested In A Man Like Me 91
Sometimes love mean having to say
   good-by 92
Although I May Wish For Younger
   Days 93
There Is A Light That I See 95
I Can See The Emotions Behind Your
   Eyes 97

If I Could Catch A Angel In Flight 98
When Emotions Run Wild 99
Although The Waters May Sometimes
   Seem Cold 101
I Know How You Feel In The Life That
   You Live 102
As I Am Sitting And Thinking About
   The Life That I Live 103
Wait And See If Life Will Be Good To
   You And Me 104
To Go From A Feeling Of Sadness To
   Being Able To Smile 105
Let Us Not Sleep The Day Away 106
When We Are Looking Through The
   Mirror What Do We See 107
When Imagination Is Lost 108
Changing Values Can Sometimes Set
   What Is Wrong Right 109
A Quiet Place For Me To Be 110
I Am In The Eye Of A Storm 111
It Is Not Your Burden To Bear 112
Every Day I Want You To Open Your
   Eyes To See 114
Our Wit's End 115
A Message For The Ones That We
   Love 116
I Am Closing My Eyes To Sleep 117
I Often Wonder If I Will Awaken In
   The Morning Light 118
Seeing Myself Everyday 119
The Time We Let Pass Us By 120
The Memories Of Your Love Live On
   In Me 121
About The Author 122

The Memories That We Leave Behind

Through the end of time and from when time did begin
You were always destined to be my friend
You may not be able to understand what you see
Don't look down on me for we may share a common destiny

A destiny that you cannot yet see but a destiny that will come to be
For one day your eyes will open to see the love that exists between you and me
Don't look down on someone you don't know
For one day your love for them may truly grow

When it is me that you see your smile will become so bright
For you begin to remember your dream of me in the night
You began to remember when we sat down to eat by candlelight
There will be a smile ever so bright when you see me in the light

Don't look down on me for there are people just like you and me
That will overcome all of the obstacles that we see
To bring about a future that we truly want to come to be
For we want to be the ones to determine our true destinies

We do not want to live our lives just to struggle to get by
We do not want to live our lives and question the reasons why
Why could we not accept the way that other people feel?
And open our hearts to share a love that can help them to heal

Through the end of time and from when time did begin
We know that in the nature of man there has been sin
We are giving a choice in how we want to be remembered in the end
Let it be with a love that people can feel just like when our lives did begin

I Am Alive With The Joy That I Can See

I am alive with the joy that I can see
How the oceans of the world are calling out to me
To come to join them in all of their majesties
To partake of all the glory that can be

To close my eyes and imagine such a feeling
To partake in a never-ending journey
To open my heart to all that I can feel
And to begin to understand the purpose of my existence

To return to the place where I used to be
That is the true journey that is calling out to me
I can feel a calling just to let go
To accept a life that I can come to know

To not be afraid to open my heart to feel
The flow of energy that the oceans give
To partake in the energy that nature gives
To feel the flow of lives that once lived

To read a word and feel it's meaning
To understand the dreams that people are dreaming
I am alive with the energy of nature
That has been flowing through us since the dawn of creation

 I can feel what we are all meant to feel
That is the flow of energy that nature has to give
There is such serenity and peace that I can feel
I am filled with the knowledge of the life that I will come to live

A Legacy Of Love

Sometimes I wonder why I am here and then the answer becomes ever so clear
For there are people that need to hear how their lives are so very dear
For there are people that cry a tear thinking that no one cares about their fear
No whisper returns to their ears letting them know someone hears
For they need to know that they are truly loved year after year

To be special in someone's eyes is what we all want to truly realize
We want to feel a love that we can trust knowing someone will be there for us
A love that can reach inside our hearts and from us will never depart
We want to be able to open our eyes to see a love that is waiting for you and me
To no longer wonder why we are here or even why we sometimes cry a tear

To cry for the people that we see who need to be loved just like you and me
For what is our reality to be? If we cannot love people we can see
If we cannot put forth a helping hand to show someone we understand
That there will be times in our lives when our lives may not go as planned

For love to be shared, love must be nurtured
Let us not wonder why we are here but know why we are here
Let us move to heal people's hearts year by year tear by tear
To accept the love in our hearts that we were given
And change the hearts of the people that are living

Let's leave a legacy of love before we depart
A legacy that will forever live in people's hearts
A legacy of the lives that we have lived
A legacy of the way that we were able to feel
A legacy of the hearts that we were able to heal

Sometimes I wonder why I am here and then the answer becomes ever so clear
For there are people that need to hear how their lives are ever so dear
For there are people that need to know that for them someone will cry a tear
Let there be a legacy of love that we are able to give year by year

Loved In Our Home

It is time that you sit down and hear me out
Before you feel the need to scream and shout
There have been times when I have been wrong
I am willing to cast aside my pride to keep our love strong

I'm sorry for everything that I have put you through
And I'm sorry about the things that you had to do
For I know that I created in you a series of doubts
Leading you to question what our love is about

I made mistakes that I am not too proud to say
Life is about mistakes that we make along the way
We can still recover and strengthen our lives every day
When we are willing to admit that we are wrong in what we do or say

When you remember everything that we have been through
Then you will understand just how much my love means to you
For our lives will never be perfect in every way
For there will always be changes in our lives every day

But before you put me down and shut me out
Think about what the love between us is all about
If you still think that the love between us is wrong
Then I guess it is time that we decide to stand alone

For if our love cannot grow strong
Then the love between us is wrong
It will be better for us to stand along
To find a love that can make us feel loved when we come home

Sometimes We Just Have To Slow Down

Sometimes we just have to slow it down
And wait for life to bring us back around
For when you believe in life the way that I do
You will understand that life brings love back to me and you

There will be changes in our lives that will always come and go
That is something that we all sooner or later come to know
When you learn to flow with the wind you will be able to start again
For when you fall, you will find the strength to get up off the ground

Whether you are rich or you are poor
You can find the courage to enter any door
We are all living in this world
Trying to find that diamond or pearl

Trying to stand up as a woman or a man
Trying to hold our heads high with faith that we can understand
Sometimes we just have to slow down
And wait for life to bring love back around

For even when we may fall down
We have the strength to get up off the ground
When we look inside our hearts
We will find that we have always had strength from the start

Sometimes we just have to slow down
To open our eyes and take a second look around
To be able to see a world that is filled with love
Just waiting for us to find the courage to dream of

Adventures That Life Will Put Us Through

Through the many adventures that life will put us through
To our dreams, it can sometimes be hard for us to remain true
For some of our dreams may be lost along the way
Never to come back to us on another day

Lost within the confines of our minds
Slipped away from us with the passage of time
But some dreams refuse to let go
That waits in the background for another chance to grow

The dreams of our hearts are still alive in us
Telling us to take a chance and in ourselves have trust
As we live our lives for only a short time
We should never be afraid of the dreams within our hearts and our minds

We should never be afraid and hold inside our hearts
The dreams that so many lives are waiting to share before we depart
We should let the dreams of our hearts lead the way
For they can help to guide the lives that come our way

Our dreams can be an ember that ignites a fire within someone's heart
Our dreams can give someone peace before they depart
Our dreams can spark their imaginations to live
For our dreams are filled with a sincerity that they can feel

For their hearts can begin to whisper that love is truly real
When a song in their hearts is what they are able to feel
Although our dreams it may be hard to remain true
We bear a responsibility to the ones that came before and after me and you

Time Of Change Upon Us

There is a time of change for us
When we are called to make decisions that we can trust
When we look out upon the world and begin to see
What we did in the past has become history

We come to know that each decision that we make
Can have a lasting effect on the road that we take
Affecting our lives in ways that we come to know
We are learning to overcome our tragedies and grow

There will be times when our frustrations will show
When it is hard for us to accept the things, we came to know
But we know that there can be a change in the air
And to that change, we cannot say that we do not care

Although changes can create doubts in our hearts
We cannot be afraid to decide the start
For we cannot keep ourselves frozen in time
Because we cannot freeze the thoughts in our minds

Changes will forever be a part of the lives that we live
The effects of the changes are what we will forever feel
For a ripple that begins in a pond
Can reflect the beautiful rays of the sun

For a ripple that begins within our hearts
Can affect our lives until the day that we depart
There will be a time of change that come upon us
Within our hearts is where we will find the love to strengthen our trust

Changes Of Minds Changes Of Hearts

Change of minds change of hearts
When one love ends another love starts
For as our emotions rise and fall
We reach out for someone to call

Forever praying that people will understand
That change will happen to every woman and man
For it seems a perfect life is not what we are meant to live
Given the range of emotions every day that we feel

Yet what else can we do?
Except try to find a path that leads us through
There will be valleys, mountains, and hills
That will rise and fall like the lives that we live

For we are always looking for something to do
That can occupy our minds and delight our hearts too
The nature of our lives is to search for the reasons that we are alive
Even if that search makes it more difficult for us to survive

To share our love, hopes, and dreams
That is more important than any pearl or diamond ring
For without love, hopes and dreams
Our lives would not mean anything

Changes of minds Changes of hearts
When one love ends another love also begins
For as our emotions will rise and fall
We know that from within our hearts love will call

Music In Me And Music In You

When you feel the need to let it all out
You don't need to be afraid to go out and shout
When you feel the need to move your body
You don't need to be afraid to let yourself party

Let yourself have a little fun
In the rain or the sun
You don't have to worry about the weather
Let your body move like a feather

Release the worries of the day
You don't need to be afraid to hear what people say
Everything that you do is up to you
Let your feelings come shining through

Living our lives is up to me and also up to you
It is time for us to accept the things that we can do
it is time to give our dreams a chance to come true
That is what means more to me and it should mean more to you

It is all in the way that we think
Whether we will swim or we will sink
It is time to release any anger or doubts we may feel
And begin to treasure the moments in the lives that we live

When we are moving our bodies to the beat of the dance
In our hearts, we are willing to take a chance
To look around at everyone that is there
To be filled with laughter and throw our hands in the air

Hearing the music coming from everywhere
Will allow us to release our feelings of care
Come on everybody take a look at us
Feeling the music in ourselves we now have trust

Never again will we be afraid to shout
And to let our feelings out
Never again will we be afraid to shout
For we know what living our lives is all about

We have opened our eyes and we can see
How music can bring our lives back into harmony
We have opened our hearts and we can feel
The precious moments that life has to give

Music in me, music in you
That is how we can feel our dreams come true
Music in me, music in you
The way that we live our lives is up to me and up to you

I Can Hear The Words That You Say

I can hear the words that you say
When you tell me that our lives will get better every day
But sometimes words can fall on deaf ears
When the actions behind the words do not appear

I have been waiting year after year
But you only leave me with a falling tear
I have been waiting for love to appear
The actions behind the words that I hear

Show me through your actions
A love shared with plenty of passion
Reflecting on the words of love that I hear
Before my love for you start to disappear

If there are no actions behind the words that you say
I wonder how our lives can get better every day
When love is not shared through your actions
I wonder how can our lives will ever be filled with plenty of passion

I can hear the words that you say
But I need you to love me just that way
I need to feel the passion that comes from your words of love
Turned into a chemical reaction that I can always dream of

Because love should cause a chemical reaction
When love is shared with plenty of passion
When you turn me on with a love so strong
You should know that you will never be left alone

For I will always stay by your side
When the love that you give takes me on a wonderful ride
When you can love me with passion
Within my heart and my body, there will always be a chemical reaction

Words That We Wonder To Say

Time is something that we sometimes let pass
For we think that time will forever last
We know that our lives will one day come to an end
We know that there will be another life ready to begin

For there are so many words that we wonder to say
Thinking about how they will affect our lives every day
So for us, time just continues to slip away
As we find ourselves waiting for another day

We can change the life that someone lives
And help their hearts begin to heal with the love we can give
Are we right to hold back the words that we want to say?
When we can change someone's life every day

When we hold back the words we wonder to say
We are preventing someone's heart from being healed every day
When we take the time to stand up and say how we feel
Maybe the words that we say can help someone's heart to heal

Time is something that we sometimes let pass us by
Only to regret the moments that we did not try
For when we see the tears in someone's eyes
We may be failing to take the moment to wipe them dry

When we kneel down and begin to pray
We want there to be wisdom in the words that we say
For we will never know the full effects of the words that we say
Until time has passed and our lives have slipped away

I Did It All For You

I did it all for you
So that your dreams could come true
I stepped aside and lowered my pride
I let the love in my heart be my guide
I turned aside from what I wanted to do
Just to give your dreams a chance to come true
I took the blame I took the shame
I allowed you to play your game

And still, I tried to honor your name
Even when I knew that your love did not reflect the same
Even when I knew that you were doing me wrong
I still let my love for you grow strong
I don't know how many men could accept what I went through
I did it all because of my love for you
I have often wondered if the shoes were on the other feet
Would your love for me also be so complete?

Would you change and admit defeat?
To feel a love that could be all so sweet
For every time that we came together
There were distant clouds from the coming weather
For your love is like the tides of the ocean
Forever coming and going with every motion
For your love for me was never embraced
From the tides of your love that I could trace

What am I going to do regarding my feelings for you?
When I know that now you need my love to be true
You need me to be in your life to help you overcome your pain and sacrifice
For there will always come a time when everyone pays a price
There is a price that I paid for you
So that your dreams would come true
Regardless of everything that you put me through
My love for you has always remained true

It Will Amaze The World

The entire world, people will be amazed to see
That there is no other person just like me
And if you ask me what my specialty is?
I would say that I blend in with other people that I see
I understand so much history
That sometimes life to me is no mystery
If you were like me you would feel your soul run free
For within your heart you would feel a love that was meant to be

You would feel the love from deep within your heart
That would allow you to create beautiful art
For the love in my heart calls out to every one of you
To accept the love that is being given to you
From the love that you will be able to feel
You will be able to treasure every day that you live
You can put aside your pride and allow loved ones to stay by your side
You have come to understand the true meaning of love and pride

For I have found out in the life that I live
That we hurt ourselves more when we push away the ones with love to give
As long as our lives are not over yet
We can still change the lives that we live before we have regrets
In the entire world, each one of us is rare
And if we open our hearts we can listen from everywhere
How love causes our hearts to sing
When we are willing to accept that love can change everything

In the entire world, there is no one else like me
But it gives me great joy when there is love in the hearts of the people that I see
The entire world, people will be amazed to see
How that precious feeling of love can change their destinies
In the entire world, there is no one else like me
But there are people that can share my destiny
When they open their hearts with the love that they can give
Then they are just like me with the compassion they feel

We Lost Someone The Other Day

We lost someone the other day
In my heart, I didn't know what to say
I just knelt down to pray
To hear a message from God that would guide my way

For when we lose someone we care about
In our hearts it makes us want to shout
For there are so many memories of the things that we use to do
Sometimes it can be hard to see our lives through

For there are memories of them being by our sides
Sharing a love that we never wanted to hide
For there are memories that we never want to let go
That has become a part of the lives that we came to know

We lost someone that used to come by and say
How are you doing? What do you want to do today?
Do you want to play some ball?
Or do you just want to sit on the wall?

We lost someone that truly did care
That each life was precious and rare
Someone for whom we let ourselves drift apart
Never truly telling them how we felt in our hearts

We lost someone the other day
In our hearts, we didn't know what to say
For we never thought how we would feel
When there are no longer here to accept the love we give

The Clicking Of Our Hearts

Back on the block looking at the clock
I saw that it was late so I didn't want to wait
You see I had a place to be and there were people to see
You would feel the same if you were me

For as I was walking down the street there was a sight so sweet
For when I saw you there I knew that we were destined to meet
For without each other our lives would be incomplete
We would always be searching for each other to make our lives complete

Listening to the sound of the beating of our hearts
We knew that we were searching to find each other from the start
We knew that there was a connection that existed between us
But we were too ashamed to give that connection our trust

We passed each other by without telling each other "hi "
And as we both passed each other we felt the tears come to our eyes
With no understanding of the reasons why we both felt like we wanted to cry
For we felt that there was a love that was about to die

As we walked our separate ways there was a voice that said,
 turn back that way
From the love in your heart do not stray for you cannot run away
For I will bring love back to you today and give you the words you need to say
For I have heard your voice when you knelt down to pray

We turned around without knowing why only feeling to give love another try
Not wanting our dreams of love to die meeting each other we could not be shy We knew that love could happen at any time regardless of the clicking of the clock
With the feelings of love in our hearts, we found the key that would turn the lock

Let Love Reach Deep Inside My Soul

I know that I am getting old
I don't want to feel old in my soul
I want to feel the love in my heart
That will be there even after I depart

I want to remember the good times
I want to remember the bad times
I want to remember so that I can look back and say
That I tried to live my life my way

I know that we all have to age
And that sometimes our lives may be written on a page
Of the things that we were able to do
And of the dreams that we were able to make come true

We all have these thoughts in our minds
For which we are seeking answers all the time
Answers to how we will feel when we grow old
Praying that there will never be a coldness that reaches into our souls

For we do not want to forget about the times when we were just a child
And how we were always willing to share our smiles
For when I grow old I want to always be able to feel
A love that can reach deeply into my soul

For every tear that falls from my eyes
Let it be from a love that I am able to recognize
For every day that I grow old
Let love live in the deepest part of my soul

When A Time Of Change Comes Upon Us

When a time of change comes upon us
We are called to make decisions that we can trust
For when we look out upon the world, we begin to see
That what we did in the past has become a part of history

For each decision that we decide to make
Can have a lasting effect on the road that we take
Affecting our lives in ways that we come to know
We are learning to overcome our tragedies and grow

There will be times when our frustrations will show
When it may be hard to accept the things that we come to know
But we can clearly see that there will be changes in the air
And from deeply within our hearts, we cannot say that we do not care

Although changes can create doubts in our hearts
Leaving us to not want to make a decision from the start
We know that we cannot keep ourselves frozen in time
Because we cannot freeze the thoughts flowing through our minds

Changes will forever be a part of the lives that we live
For the effects of the changes is what we will forever feel
For a ripple that begins in a pond
Can reflect the beautiful rays of the sun

For a ripple that begins in our hearts
Can continue to affect our lives from the start
When the time of change comes upon us
Within our hearts is where we will find a courage, we can trust

To See Beyond The Veils Of Time

*To see beyond the veils of time
To finally unravel the mysteries of the mind
we are able to look back to the past
We can finally understand our lives at last
To see the connections between you and me
We can finally accept what was meant to be
Through the eyes of each other we are able to see
The many emotions revealed to you and me*

*There will be no more running away from who we are
Of letting life stop us from reaching for a star
For whether we are born rich or we are born poor
In the winds of time we can soar
For the many lives that were hidden from us
are revealed in the memories that we can trust
For with the clarity of thoughts within our minds
We open our hearts to the memories that we can find*

*Never again will we feel alone
For our hearts and minds have become strong
For the past, present and the future
Tells us that in our lives there is always a solution
When we open our hearts and minds to what we can be
We can change the realities of you and me
To see beyond the veils of time
The extraordinary events unfold in our hearts and minds*

*To take away our feelings of sorrow
and to open our eyes to the dawn of a beautiful tomorrow
For when we open our hearts to everything that is surrounding us
We can finally begin to understand that it is ourselves we must first trust
To see beyond the veils of time
To finally unravel the mysteries of the mind
We can open our eyes and look back upon the past
So that we may see the road that has been revealed to us at last*

Looking On The Inside Of You

Looking on the inside of you
That is something that I seek to do
With everything that life will put me through
I need to know that I can always count on you
There are times when it may seem like my life is hard
There are times when it may seem like I am being torn apart
During those times I pray that I can find
The love that still lives in my heart and mind

For there are many times when our lives get hard
And our relationships gets torn apart
Financial and emotional distress
Can put our relationships to the test
Bringing out our frustrations
Leaving us with a feeling of desperation
With a feeling of being on the outside looking in
We can feel that our tears will never end

Yet our tears can mean that we are either happy or sad
For the tears that we cry do not always mean that we are mad
It can be just a single tear that someone notice when they are near
Or it can be a flood of tears that we have been holding back for years
Looking on the inside of you
That is something that I seek to do
For looking on the inside of you
I want to know the problems that life is putting you through

For I am not heartless in the way that I feel
I am not selfish in the love that I give
For I know that life can bring out our tears
I know about the pain and suffering that can last for years
Looking on the inside of you that is something that I seek to do
For I want to be there to help make your dreams come true
On the outside looking in is where I will begin
For I want to strengthen our lives with a love that will never end

Imagine Yourself Being His Age

Imagine yourself being his age
Never having your name written on a page
No one to say that you have ever been here
No one for you to ever cry a tear
To reach out with all of their hearts
To let you feel their love before you depart
To remind you that you was once a child
And how you had such a beautiful smile

Little child come with me
Let's open his eyes to a love that he can see
Let's open his heart to a love that he can feel
So that he may treasure the remaining life that he has to live
Little child come with me
Open the eyes of the old man that you see
For he is lost and alone
And need someone to guide him home

When we are searching for something to hold on to
We are searching for something inside of you and me
We are searching for something that we can feel
To help us to treasure the lives that you live
We are searching for a hope and a dream
That can help us to define what our lives can mean
We are searching for something that we want to be real
We are searching to feel the love that someone can give

Imagine yourself being his age
Never having your name written on a page
No one to say that you have ever been here
No one for you to ever cry a tear
To reach out with all of their hearts
To let you feel their love before you depart
To remind you that you was once a child
And how you had such a beautiful smile

To Walk Along The Beach

To walk along the beach
To see your dreams within reach
To feel that your life is getting better
You can feel the changing weather
You can feel that a storm has passed
And your heart begin to heal at last
For as you take each breath of fresh air
You can now see how much you care

About everything that you see
From the people that you love and even me
For I was someone that passed you by
You took the first step and told me, "hi"
You turned my frown into a smile
When you stopped and talked to me for a while
You made my walk along the beach
An adventure for which I should seek

For a dream can become real
When someone guides you in the life that you live
I was glad that you walked along the beach
And that you came within my reach
For you also made me believe
That my dreams could also be achieved
That every breath of fresh air
Can bring to me someone that care

So now as I walk along the beach
I can feel that my dreams are within reach
Life never ending cycle of how we change the way we care
When someone comes along and makes us aware
That when we least expect it for us someone will be there
For life will bring someone within our reach that truly care
They will be able to join us along our journey as we walk along the beach
And we will know in our hearts that one day our destinies we will reach

Turnaround Faces Changing Places

Turnaround faces changing places
Emotions that start heartbeats races
Emotions that we feel inside
Emotions that we sometimes cannot hide
Emotions breaking down our pride
Removing the doubts that we are ready for that ride
For there will always be a need for someone to be by our side
For their love we will lower our pride

We can be afraid someone that we love will turn away
When we need them to love us every day
When we need them to open their hearts to hear what we have to say
To stand together when hard times come our way
We need them to put themselves in our shoes
To understand how in love we can win or lose
To understand why they are the ones that we choose
And why our love they should never abuse

Turnaround faces changing places
There are times in our hearts when love erases
Turnaround faces changing places
Emotions start heartbeats racing
Hearing their voices there can be a sudden scare
Wondering if the ones that we love will still be there
Hearing their cries and hearing their tears
Will their love stand strong for us through the years?

Tragedy strikes tears of pain
There are some things that can drive us insane
For we know that in the lives that we live we need to search within
We are not perfect we sometimes commit sin
Yet we can change the lives of every woman and man
When it is each other we try to understand
Turnaround faces changing places
We can treasure each moment and tender embrace

A Simple Thought Flows Through My Mind

*A simple thought flows through my mind
Whatever happened to all of the time?
For it seemed like it was only yesterday
When I was born in the world today
When I let out my first tear
The price for entering the world this year
I can still remember the feeling of being held in my mother's arms
Knowing that I was safe from any harm*

*I never thought that feeling would ever end
As I think back to when my life first did begin
I have often wondered if my life has begun as an expression of love
For that is often what I want to dream of
Not just the love of a physical nature
But the kind of love shared with all of creation
A love that can forever live in a heart
That will never from the heart depart*

*The moment when I was first born the world changed around me
Even though my eyes were not yet open to see
I am sure that my life has brought about a change in the world
For I have had contact with so many boys and girls
Truly so many people have felt the love that I had to give
A love that in their hearts will forever live
Passed on from generation to generation
Love passed on since the dawn of creation*

*A simple thought flows through my mind
How precious is a love that can transcend time?
How precious is the love given to us?
How precious is a heart that is given in trust?
When the birth of a child can change the world
Their gift of love is worth more than any diamond or pearl
A simple thought flows through my mind
Precious is our lives and the love that we share over the passage of time*

The Things That You Did Wrong

Maybe you think that I can't take
All of the trouble that you decide to make
Maybe you think that I did you wrong
Why to me you continually try to hold on
I did everything that a man was supposed to do
Just to keep your love for me true
But I can see at last that you are still holding on to love from your past
I can see it in your eyes your love for another that you always try to hide

I am not blind to what I see that is why there are so many changes in me
So many emotions running wild that is why sometimes you don't see me smile
For the love that you give to me is not the way it is supposed to be
When what you think, is that I did wrong
Then why to me you continually try to hold on
With everything that I did for you still your love for me did not remain true
For you kept someone's else love inside of you
And you made me pay just for loving you

Maybe you think that I can't take all of the things that you put me through
Then again you do not know everything that life has already put me through
Maybe you think that I can't take all of the trouble that you decide to make
Maybe you think that I did you wrong that is why sometimes you feel so alone
I did everything that a man was supposed to do just to keep your love for me true
But I can see at last that you are still holding on to a love from your past
I can sometimes see it in your eyes
Your love for another that you always try to hide

I know that sooner or later the truth will come out
To either confirm or disclaim all of my doubts
For there were so many that I was able to see
That allowed me to accept what was going on around me
Maybe you are wrong if you think that I cannot take
The decisions that you finally decide to make
Maybe it is time that you think again
How do you want love in your life to begin and end

When You Least Expect Something Happens

When you least expect it something happens to put a smile on your face
A tender moment placed in your heart that may never be erased
With such a feeling in your heart you are filled with so much pride
For you are finally able to see that you can let your heart decide
For through all of the anger that can turn people into strangers
You know that you can't deny the love that you feel
And turn away from a love that you know can be real
For when you least expect it something can make you smile

You can see something that makes you sit down and think for a while
That the anger that you sometimes feel can change the life that you live
Taking away the love that people were willing to give
Leaving you to wonder about the life that you live
For when you let the anger that you feel turn the ones that love you into strangers You are allowing the anger that you feel to turn you away from what can be real
When you least expect it something can make you smile
You see something that makes you sit down and think for a while

You will be able to open your heart to the changes that life gives
For we are given a chance to be renewed in body and soul
For that is something that we are able to see every day that we grow old
For when we thought that we had seen everything
Suddenly in our hearts we feel to sing
For along comes something that can change how we feel
Opening our hearts to dream every day that we live
For the love that we have always been longing to feel

Opening our hearts to dream again of the smile that can bring tears to our eyes
There is so much love in the world that we can suddenly realize
We can begin again to treasure every day that we are alive
For the love that we feel helps us to treasure each moment that we live
For the moment will appear and then the moment will disappear
Leaving us with a love that causes us to cry our tears
For when we least expect it life will bring the moment back again
Giving us another chance to feel at peace in the lives that we live

When we let the moment pass us by we will only turn around and cry
For we were afraid to take a chance and we let our dreams die
That is why we can never neglect the moment when it will appear

For the moment can bring us a happiness that will last from year to year
Smile a beautiful smile and every moment will be as precious to you as it is to me
We cannot let this moment pass for it was meant to bring together you and me
When we deny the way that we feel we deny the love that we can give
We cannot deny the love that is beating in our hearts we cannot remain apart

When we least expect it something happens to put a smile on our faces
A tender moment placed in our hearts that may never be erased
With such a feeling in our hearts we are filled with so much pride
For we are finally able to see that we can let our hearts decide
For through all of the anger that can turn people into strangers
We know that we can't deny the love that we feel
And turn away from a love that we know we can give
For when we least expect it something can happen that is so wonderful and real

I Am Just A Child

When I was a child I was asked," What do I want to be?"
I smiled and said," I am just a child, I will just wait and see."
For being a child I had all the time in the world
For there was so much for me to learn I was just a little boy or a girl
With no worries of the mind just the thought of play all the time
To awake every day with something to say that will always be a child's way
To want to sparkle in the light with a smile ever so bright
To look up at the moon to imagine the fork chasing the spoon

To never see a dull moment for a child seeks an opponent
To show how smart they can be they jump for joy that you are able to see
When I was a child I wanted to travel the world to feel the love of a beautiful girl
I believed that nothing could hurt me for I had x-ray eyes to see
You ask me," What do I want to be?" I want to be superman if you ask me
Yet back to the realities of the day where I have to accept what may come my way
I know now that whatever life may bring I pray there will always be a song to sing
For in my heart I want there to be a song of love that can truly enchant me

With dreams that will one day allow me to enter into the heavens above
I am a child and I want to always be able to smile
I want someone to be able to look at me and see the beauty inside of me
And if I have a fear I want someone to always be near
I want someone to hear and to come and dry my tear
For I can be just a boy or I can be just a girl
But with the love in my heart I can bring love to the world
Do you not see that I am more precious than any diamond or pearl?

If I was not here then you would truly need to fear
For the sounds of laughter and love would never reach your ear
For there would never be a child's voice that you would ever again hear
Without the hearing of a child's voice every man and woman should cry a tear
For that would be the beginning and the ending of the world
When our lives are not filled with the love and laughter of boys and girls
You ask me," Why am I here?" I am here to bring love to the world
So your heart will be able to open to receive the fulfillment of God's gift of love

Never Mind What Was Said Yesterday

Never mind what was said," yesterday" for that day has slipped away
For life will always bring a change our way with the words that we say
Never mind what happened in the past for that was the way that we felt last
For we can change in the blink of an eye from a feeling of joy to a tear that we cry
We scream and we shout and then we want to hang out
We are still trying to figure out what loving each other is about
That is a part of the lives that we live when we are changing the way that we feel
From Love to hate our feelings keep changing alone the road that we take

We come together to share the love in our hearts then we sometimes break apart
You see, we are just here for today knowing that our lives change along the way
We can be gone tomorrow for there is no time that we can borrow
Leaving behind the memories that was shared with the ones that we cared
We say words that we do not mean, we do not mean to deny each other's dreams
Never mind what was said," yesterday" for that day has slipped away
For we are still able to change today with the words that we now say
Starting from this moment in time let's talk about what is on our hearts and minds

We can bring out the love that can help to heal one another
We can show each other how we feel with the love that we are willing to give
We may think that we are too late so we may think to continue to hesitate
As long as we are willing to cast aside our pride we can be by each other's side
For as long as we are able to breathe there is love that we can receive
A love for which we have been waiting to feel can finally find a home
In these changing times it is hard for us to understand our hearts and our minds
Yet we are being asked, to share the love in our hearts and minds all the time

It is time for us to come to the realization that every decision can be a mistake
For there are alternate decisions that could have changed the roads that we take
We should not look back on the past and regret the decisions that we made last
For if we begin to regret our decisions then in ourselves we can begin to lose trust

Never mind what was said," yesterday" for that day has slipped away
For life will always bring a change our way with the words that we say
We have to stay strong in our hearts least our lives begin to drift apart
Let's share each moment with the love that springs from our hearts and minds

It Is Okay to Say Good-Bye

It's okay to say good-bye to the ones that you love
It's okay to let their spirits soar and enter into heaven's door
It's okay to say how you feel so that your heart can begin to heal
When destiny calls out our names what more in our lives can we ever claim
Time to forgive the blame and the shame and accept when destiny calls our
names It is time to find the peace that we seek that we can forever keep
For it is time that we let the ones that we love go in peace
To find a place where their struggles have forever ceased

For us they leave behind their memories of love
As our faith is strengthened in the belief of the heavens above
We can find happiness in the joy of how they will feel
And contentment in the knowledge that they will watch over us as we live
For it is okay for us to say good-bye even with the tears that we cry
For that is the way that we feel for the love that they were able to give
For they touched our lives in so many ways
How could we not love them for the love that they gave?

For we will cry our tears for as long as our hearts need to heal
For it can take us a long time to forget the way that we feel
I don't mean the love that they were able to give
For the pain of losing them, may be what we still feel
Yet we should not burden them with the way that we feel
For they may be looking down on us praying that our hearts will heal
For we should feel a happiness that their pain and suffering will no longer be
Unless we cause them to feel sadness when they look down on you and me

We should let them go with happiness in our hearts
Knowing that there will come a time when we will also depart
For there is a chance that we will one day meet them again
For within our hearts they have become more than just friends
They helped us to understand that our lives must go on
That the bonds of love can stay forever strong
It is okay for us to say good-bye with the tears that we cry
For one day we may meet them again and share a love that will never end

Here Is A Prayer From Me

Here is a prayer from me that I pray I will one day come to see
For my thoughts are sometimes not right I chose the darkness instead of the light
It was an unconscious choice a choice that took away my voice
For the pain that I would earn to me was of great concern
And I pray that I am able to forgive the things that I had to do to live
May my eyes be open to see that I can make a change in me
Although it is hard for me to forgive myself
If I can't forgive myself then how can anyone else

This is a prayer from me that I may one day open my eyes to see
That I can forgive the things that I do
With an understanding that I can make mistakes too
That I am not a perfect man within my heart this is what I need to understand
To not give up the things that I try to do whether or not my dreams will come true
To be able to accept the mistakes I will make along the road of life that I take
To be able to overcome the obstacles in the road
And to be able to accept the weight of my load

For I know that there were times when I did wrong
And in my heart, I felt so isolated and alone
But I knew that I had the strength in me to grow strong
As I lowered my head and headed back home
I knew that I had to strength to change
For the way that I felt I didn't want to remain the same
For I wanted to be able to lift my head high
And not feel to cry when people passed me by

Here is a prayer from me that I pray I may one day come to see
For my thoughts are sometimes not right I chose the darkness instead of the light
It was an unconscious choice a choice that took away my voice
For the pain that I would earn to me was of great concern
I still had hope for I knew that I could be saved by God's grace
For deep within my heart, it was God's love that I now chose to embrace
And I pray that one day God will send his Angels to me
This is a prayer from me that I pray will one day come to be

It Is The Morning Of Another Day

It is the morning of another day
To prepare our minds for what will come our way
To open our hearts and truly hear what people have to say
So that they may feel at peace when they feel their lives drifting away
For we can leave them with such a feeling
That every moment is precious to be living
That every moment their hearts will be able to feel
That they will be loved every moment they live

To me every life is precious and so very rare
I may not have known you but your life I still care
I know that in every heart there is a love so sweet
That calls out to all the people that they meet
For with love we call out to each other
Trying to bring peace to the hearts of one another
Like when we close our eyes to dream
We want to dream of love as an expression of what our lives mean

To be able to see a smile upon each other's face
Should bring to us a tear that we can trace
For the feeling of caring that we are able to see
Can reflect the love inside of the hearts of you and me
We are not alone in the pain and sorrow that we may sometime feel
For we see that in the lives that other people also live
In our hearts we have to learn to let go of our sorrow
For God promises us that there will be a better tomorrow

Each of us have a different pain that we claim
There is also a feeling of love calling our names
Some time for us to remember the love in our hearts we have to forgive
The mistakes that we made in the lives that we live
We sometimes need to release the pain that we feel
To feel the love that people are willing to give
It is the morning of another day
On my knees I will get down and pray

That in every one of our lives and love will find its way
That each of us will be able to feel the love for which we pray
I may not know you and you may not know me
But still in my heart and on my knees, I pray
That the Kingdom of God you may one day see
For when the love of God set each of our souls free
We are given the chance to experience a true reality
For it is the morning of a new day when God has sent his Angels to guide our way

Could You Ever Imagine The Face You Will See

Could you ever imagine that the face you would see
Would change the way that your life would come to be
Could you imagine a face seen in a dream
Would change what living your life could mean
For seeing a face sparked a fire in your heart
That would forever burn even after you depart
For the visions of you were able to see
Reached out to affect the heart of me

Making me finally able to realize how each of our hearts
Can be connected from the very start
For the face that was revealed to you
Changed your heart and put you on a path that was true
There is an excitement in your eyes
That is very easy to recognize
The sign of a heart that is truly touched
When it receives what it has been longing for so much

For you received a sign that your life was truly rare
When the face appeared seemingly out of nowhere
The face filled with a love that would forever be true
Reached out and touched the very heart of you
Your sudden rush of tears the release of all of your fears
A moment that will live in your heart for the rest of your years
For as you closed your eyes you begun to pray
Thank-you! Lord! For the blessings given to you on this day

Out of all the people living upon the earth
Praying to understand the reasons of their birth
You were chosen to finally be able to see
A face that reflects a love so bright
That every one of us will cry our tears at its sight
You could never imagine how the face that you would see
Would touch the hearts of you and me
And change everything that we would ever see

Can you imagine every heart that you have ever touched?
And how many lives have you changed so much?

For your reflection can be seen in the love that you were able to give
For the many lives that will reflect your love in the lives that they live
Ever so lightly is the feeling of the hearts that you have touched
For the sight of your smile and the love that you gave came to mean so much
Can you ever imagine that the face that you would see
Could turn out to show you that there could be peace in the hearts of you and me

A Love Story Once Told

I have to go back down the road
To find a story that once was told
A story of a love that was ever so true
That was once revealed to me and to you
There are only the fragments left behind
Of a love that once lived in the hearts of yours and mine
I pray that I will see you back in time
For the fragments of love you also need to find

For the memories that we left behind
Can help us to remember why we should always be kind
We can go back to capture the love that we used to feel
So that our hearts will remain true to the love that we can give
For to ourselves we can always remain true
When we let love be reflected in what we say and do
And if we need to go back down that road
Surely, we can bear the burden of that load

For what we will be able to achieve
Will lighten our hearts and give us back our dreams
To live our lives with a feeling of love and care
And to see our love reach out to people everywhere
We have to go back down that road
For it leads us back to a story once told
How the fragments of our lives can be brought back together
With the love that once lived in the hearts of yours and mine

To open our eyes to the dreams that can come true
When love can be seen in the reflections of what we say and do
I have to go back down the road
To find a story that once was told
A story of a love that was ever so true
That was once revealed to me and to you
For the story that was once revealed to me and you
Revealed that our love would one day come true

Your Temper's Too High

Take it down a notch your temper's too high
Release the anger that you feel into the sky
Take it down a notch your tempers too high
That will only leave you with the tears that you cry
I know that there is anger in your heart
That may linger and begin to tear you apart
It is time to let that anger vanish in the air
To be replaced with a love that you can care

Time and time again your anger may begin
But your anger can also come to an end
For keeping the anger in your heart
Will never let you begin to heal from the start
When it comes to the life that you want to live
Is it anger that you always want to feel?
Keeping the anger because you cannot forgive
That is no way that you should want to live

For the anger that lives in your heart
Can tear your life apart
For no one wants to be near
When it is the anger that they will hear
Do you want the ones that you love to stay away from you?
To not be there to help you with what you are going through?
Do you want the ones that you love to have a fear?
That it will only be the anger from you that they will hear?

Think about the things that you will say and do
Think about the anger inside of you
Think about the way that you make the ones that you love feel
When you let the anger in your heart lives
Take it down a notch your tempers too high
Take a step back before you let your words fly
Release the anger that you feel into the sky
Let the words of love from your heart bring tears to your eye

Come Go With Me To Another World

Come go with me to another world
I can be your boy and you can be my girl
I can open your heart and let you see
That I can change how your life will come to be
I will open your heart and you will see
That you can bring out the love in me
For the way that you can make me feel
you can make my imaginations become real

For love is not something that I want to steal
I want to feel the love that someone is willing to give
For when love is given truly from the heart
Love can live forever even after we depart
You can be my diamond or you can be my pearl
For every time that I see you, you brighten up my world
For every time that I see you my heart begin to race
For I can feel a love that can transcend time and space

I know that you will be able to feel
A tingling sensation for a love that can be real
For when you look deep inside your heart
You will see that my love has always been there from the start
I knew your love from the moment of my birth
For I felt your presence upon the earth
And that it would only be a matter of time
Before your heart reached out to touch mine

When you look at me you will be able to see
That our love was meant to be
For we were connected through time and space
Calling out to each other to meet at a special place
Come and go with me to another world
I can be your boy and you can be my girl
And together with the love that we share we can change the world
With a love that is worth more than diamonds or pearl

Differences In The Lives That We Live

I'm trying to make a difference in the lives that we live
I'm trying to change the way that you sometimes make me feel
I'm not a superman who can let the words fly by
I'm only a man who have the heart to always want to try
But there are times when you turn away from me in the night
If you could look into my heart, you would know that you were not right
You would see the pain that lingers until the night
That would not go away even in the morning light

You were leaving a pain in my heart
That would let you know that you were tearing my heart apart
For there can be so much pain that the eyes sometimes can never see
That can slowly take away the love from the hearts of you and me
I'm trying to make a difference in the lives that we live
I'm trying to change the way that I sometimes feel
I'm trying to heal the pain that can come from the past
So that I may strengthen a relationship that I know can last

For there are times when you need to open your eyes and see
That no matter what life put me through I still have to be me
For if I was to change to the way that you want me to feel
Then I would have become you and lost the essence of me
That is why it will always be that you will remain you and I will remain me
For that is how our lives were meant to be
I' m trying to make a difference in the lives that we live
It is up to you to try and understand the way that I feel

It is up to me to determine how I want my life to come to be
For after all I am the one to comprehend what I am able to see
Even though I cannot look through your eyes and see what you see
I am always willing to try and reconcile the differences between you and me
I am trying to make a difference in the lives that we live
I am trying to always understand the way that you feel
I cast aside my pride sometimes to try and reconcile the differences between us
For love is an emotion that requires us to always be willing to strengthen our trust

You Know That I Have Always Been There For You

You know that I have always been there for you
Through everything that life has put you through
Even when I knew that you were doing me wrong
Still my love for you remained very strong
So many times, I lifted you up
though the hard times I never gave up
I can remember the first time that we met
Standing in the rain at me you became upset

Wanting to control everything that I wanted to do
I had no idea of what you would put me through
Yet I held strong in the love that I did feel
For I believed that the love that we shared were real
Yet there were many changes that happened to us along the way
That continued to live in our hearts every day
Like the feelings of a past love that we can sometimes think of
When it should be each other that we should have always been thinking of

Clouded hearts in the rains of love's desires
Affecting our relationships and burning us with fire
Uncontrollable feelings that we should have left in the past
So that we could feel a happiness that could last
Still one can turn away and do what they know is wrong
And in the end break a trust that once was strong
You wonder why sometimes you may feel alone
That is because in your heart you know what you did was wrong

Yet there is a forgiveness that can be found in a heart of love
If that is what someone is truly in need of
If they are willing to put the past aside so that love can survive
Then there can be a sincere change of heart that can keep love alive
But if from that love there continues to be no passion
Then down the road there will be a chain reaction
Clouded hearts in the rains of love's desires
Can leave the breaking of hearts and the tears that burns like fire

Another Year Has Come And Gone

Another year has come and gone
So many years I have been out on my own
I know that I have to be strong
Even when events in my life start to go wrong
Sometimes the way that we feel we have to think about twice
For everyone around us will not always treat us nice
Too many times with the tears that we are crying
We sit down and start to think about the dreams that are dying

Trying to forget about what is going down
Especially when we feel ourselves falling to the ground
For there is no one to lift us up there is no one around
For the crying of our tears is the only sound
Yet the seconds, minutes and hours pass by
We let them pass with no understanding why
They are but moments in the lives that we live
That seem to forever test our strength of will

Yet we know that we must continue to live on
To try and make our hearts become strong
We can continue to try and find a better way
As we keep in our minds that we are not promised another day
We live our lives one moment at a time
With whatever peace we are able to find
When we hold on to the memories of when we were a child
When our lives get hard, we will still be able to smile

In our hearts we will never be alone
For the memories of our love remain very strong
Memories of our love will keep us strong when we are apart
Until we can get back together to share the love in our hearts
Another year has come and gone
But we know where our hearts truly belong
For in each other's hearts our love will always find a home
And as each day passes us by, we know that we will never be alone

You Are Not A Child Why Do You Cry?

You are not a child, why do you cry?
I will tell you the truth and I will not lie
I cry for the way that I feel
When I do not understand the way that I live
For when I awake each day
I search to find my way
I never know what to expect
I only know that my life is not over yet

For I am still able to feel
The love that someone is willing to give
For I am still able to smile
With someone who will talk to me for a while
I still have my family and friends
I appreciate the things they send
I appreciate their thoughts of me
Remembrance of a love that used to be

I am not a child but I still cry
For the love that I seek to feel until the day that I die
And as I walk down the hall
I turn around when I hear my name being called
Just to hear my name being called out
Makes me want to scream and shout
There is someone that cares what my life is about
That can help me to work my feelings out

I cry a tear for the way that I feel
For I know that there is a reason why I still live
To share the life that I live and the way that I feel
To help someone's heart begin to heal
For they can see me having went through so much
Still willing to share the love that can mean so much
For I am still able to see all the people around me
And how I am able to change how people's lives will come to be

Just to be able to put a smile on their faces
Will be the moments that I can embrace
I can still see the reason why I still live
That is for the love that I can still make people feel
I am no longer a child but I still cry

For I can begin the healing of a heart of someone passing me by
I cry for the way that I am able to feel
When I am able to give someone the love that they need to live

You are not a child, why do you cry?
I will tell you the truth and I will not lie
I cry for the way that I feel
When I do not understand the way that I live
For when I awake each day
I search to find my way
I never know what to expect
I only know that my life is not over yet

You Heard Some Bad News

I know that you heard some bad news that broke you down to tears
But there is one thing that I want you to remember
From the month of January to December
That I will always stand by you through the years
I will be here when you cry a tear
I will never be far I will always be near
When life treats you bad and leaves you feeling sad
Know that I will always love you more than your mom or dad

For you is the center of my universe
And what I say to you I don't need to rehearse
For the words come from deep within my soul
Know that I will love you every day that I grow old
I know that you heard some bad news that made you sad
Just remember that I will always love you more than your mom or your dad
I do not say these words in doubt
But from my heart I proudly shout

For let it be known that the seeds of love have grown
For it is how precious your love that I have come to know
For I will stand beside you through thick and thin
I will stand by you rather you lose or you win
For I know of the pain that you sometimes claim
And in your heart how you sometimes bear the blame
And how you cry your tears from a feeling of shame
Remember that I will not deny my love when I hear your name

The way that you feel I can understand
For I am not a newborn baby born in this land
Bad news is what we will sometimes hear
Leaving in our eyes the crying of our tears
But know that I will be there with you through the years
To try and comfort you with the love that I can give
For I want you to know how precious is the lives that we live
No matter what hardships we have to go through I will always be there for you

Little Child Come With Me

Little child come with me open the eyes of the old man that you see
For he is lost and alone and he need someone to guide him home
He is cold from the freezing weather it seems like he has been there forever
No one seems to want to look upon his face afraid of the tears that leaves it's traces

For to see him your feelings will never be erased
Wanting to reach out to him and give him a tender embrace
Surely you can see what I see and feel what I feel
When it comes to the love that he needs to live

Little child do not be afraid because of the clothes that he wears
For the clothes that he has to wear has such wear and tear
But his life is as precious as can be for within his heart that is what I see
We cannot judge him by the way that he look we do not know the road that he took

Cobble stones or dirt road is where he has carried the burden of his load
Do not be afraid to ask him why there are sometimes tears in his eyes
Do not be afraid to dry his tears for he needs someone to love him dear
Imagine yourself being his age never having your name written on a page

No one to say that you have ever been here and no one for you to ever cry a tear
Reach out with all of your heart and let him feel loved before he depart
Remind him that he once was a child and how he had such a beautiful smile
Little child come with me let's open his eyes to a love that he can see
Let's open his heart to a love he can feel so that he may treasure the life that he live

If we do not reach out to the old man then who will?
For in our hearts we have such a feeling of love and care to give
It is our love and care that the old man needs to feel

For we are the ones that can make a difference in his life
For we can help to ease his pain and his sacrifice

We can never deny the love that we can give
When it comes to a troubled heart that needs our love to live
Little child come with me open the eyes of the old man that you see
For he is lost and alone and he need someone to guide him home
His life is so very precious to you and to me
And we can't afford to turn away from what we see

Turnaround Faces Changing Places

Turnaround faces changing places
Emotions that start heartbeat races
Emotions that we feel inside
Sometimes we cannot hide
Emotions breaking down our pride
Doubts that we are ready for that ride
Needing someone to be by our side
For love we lower our pride

Afraid someone that we love will turn away
Needing them to love us every day
To open their hearts to what we have to say
To stand together when hard times come our way
To put themselves in our shoes
To understand how in love we can win or lose
To understand why they are the ones that we choose
And why our love they should never abuse

Turnaround faces changing places
Sometimes in our hearts love erases
Turnaround faces changing places
Emotions start heartbeat races
Hearing their voices a sudden scare
Will the ones that we love still be there
Hearing their cry hearing their tears
Will their love stand strong through the years

Tragedy strikes tears of pain
There are some things that can drive us insane
Search within where love begin
We are not perfect we sometimes commit sin
Yet we can change every woman and man
When it is each other we try to understand
Turnaround faces changing places
We can treasure each moment and tender embraces

Memories Of A Love That I Used To Feel

Memories of a love that I used to feel
Memories of a love that once was real
Memories that are still living in my heart
Filling my dreams from the start
I reach out for a love that once was there
I reach out finding only empty air
For the love that I was searching for was no longer there
the love that I still care left me to feel only empty air

Reaching out for a love that was near
Within my heart I was left with only fear
For so many times I reached out with my heart
Only to have my heart torn apart
For so many times I wanted to feel
A love that was precious and real
Only to be once again turned away
With an expression of tears from the words that I did hear

as times passed there was a change in the love that I did feel
There was a change in the love that I was willing to give
Memories of a love that I used to feel
May live in my heart for as long as I shall live
Memories of a love that I use to feel
Gave me the strength to overcome my fears
And to reach out to others with the love that I can give
For I was finally able to feel a love that turned out to be real

For when I believe that I am worthy of love
Then I will begin to feel the true meaning of love
That love starts from deep into our hearts
Reaching out to everyone that wishes to share a part
Memories of a love that I used to feel
Memories of a love that once was real
Changed the feelings that was in my heart
For my memories of love is my salvation from the star

As The River Runs Fast Like The Memories Of The Past

As the river will run fast like the memories of the past
We sometimes never look back on what we did last
We let go of the memories that we should hold close
memories of a love that we need the most
As the river flows so do the thoughts within our minds
Moving ever so swiftly with the passage of time
Thoughts of pain and thoughts of love
Mixed with the dreams that we dream of

Like a stone thrown into the water
The waves that are created are too small for us to see
We are born upon the earth to change each other's destinies
We open our eyes to see at last that we cannot separate our lives from
the past For a single memory can flow from the hearts of you and me
Affecting so many lives that are yet to be
As the water is sometimes blocked behind a dam
Our memories are sometimes blocked behind what we see

For us to reconcile what happens in our lives every day
Our memories need to flow even if they need to find another way
For we cannot let ourselves or let our minds stand still
We cannot allow anyone to gain control of our wills
We cannot let ourselves get caught up in what people say that we can do
For they are unable to look inside of the hearts of me and you
We have in our hearts and minds to become so much more
We just need to search within our hearts and find a key to open another door

When we think about all of the things that we are able to do
We can see that there are so much more to the lives of me and you
There are times when we may limit ourselves to what people say
Those are the times when we find difficulty to find our ways
As the river will run fast like the memories of the past
We sometimes never look back on what we did last
Yet our memories are what guide us along our way
That is why the past will always reflect back to our lives every day

Walking Down That Dusky Road

Walking back down that dusky road I begun to think about what I was told
That there was a greatness that I could achieve If I just had the heart to believe
I was told to look inside myself and see the truth of the great things that I could do
They told me, son, don't hide behind your fear
For there are words from your heart that people have been waiting to hear
They made me open my eyes to see to think about how my life could be
For maybe it is time that people will open their hearts to hear
The words of love that has the power to bring out their tears

Walking back down that dusty road
I thought that maybe I could help to ease people's loads
To give them something that they could feel
So that they would open their hearts with the love that they could give
That was something that I really needed to think about
For the sharing of our love is truly what living our lives should be about
Memories of what I was told lingered in my heart every day that I grew old
Walking back down that dusty road brought back memories worth more than gold

You can believe that I felt a tear fall down even as my next foot hit the ground
Tears for what I was feeling inside of a love that I should no longer hide
For I would be able to share a love that people could feel
I would be able to share a love that I was meant to give
For it is love people need to truly feel to help them to change the life they live
For I could not see how someone would not want to help someone to heal
There are so many hearts broken because they do not feel loved
That is something that no one ever dream of

From the moment that I knew there was something that I could say
That could help to heal the lives of the people that came my way
I was ready and willing to share the love that I could give
For we all deserve to feel loved in the lives that we live
And just maybe I could change the way that they feel
To help them to treasure the moments of love that life has to give
From this moment I will treasure the life that I live
And I will take great pride in the love that I can give

It Is Time To Wipe The Tears From Your Eyes

It's time to wipe the tears from your eyes
And to remember the dreams that made you believe you could fly
To stop asking yourself why and to stop being afraid to try
To stop letting time keep slipping away listening to what other people say
To go out and take a chance for the least you can do is try
Even if you do not succeed and a tear falls from your eye
To keep letting time slip away with nothing to do or to say
That is not the way that you want to be remembered some day

Don't let time keep slipping away
For in the life that you live there is love that you can feel
Don't let time slip away without sharing the love that you can give
For the love that you can give can help someone to heal
You can't be afraid to open your eyes and see
For time is slipping away from you and from me
For we can change the way that our lives are meant to be
When we share the love in our hearts with the people that we see

Time and time again you may have turned away from the people that you see
Only to find out in the end that you were actually turning away from me
For my situation in life may change from day to day
And throughout my day I may not look the same way
Maybe you may think that it may be my fault
That I may not have had the strength to achieve the dreams that I had sought
Looking at the true me you may never be able to see
Unless you take a chance to get to know me

I was a child just like you born in a world where dreams can come true
When you look a little deeper then you have become a seeker
Someone that will be able to look upon someone's face
And see the years have left its trace
It is time to wipe the tears from your eyes
And to remember the dreams that made you believe you could fly
It is time that you look inside of someone else's heart
And see that their dreams can be the same as you from the start

Will You Smile When You Hear

*Will you smile when you hear
Love is so perfect love is so clear
When love is so good love is understood
By the people in the hood
When everything that you do
Leads people back to you
From the words of love that you hear
Can't you feel the falling of a tear*

*Oooh oooh love is so good
When you move like you should
You will feel the joy in your life
That can ease your pain and your sacrifice
You no longer need to toss and turn
With the problems that you have concern
For the answers will come to you
With a love that will see you through*

*When you toss and turn in the night
You need to let the love in your heart shine bright
For within your heart there is so much that you want to say
It is time that you let the love in your heart lead the way
For there is no need for words to sometimes lead the way
When you let your body express what you want to say
Sooner or later everyone will see
How love has brought you into harmony*

*An expression of love that is beyond control
Can reach out to touch everyone's soul
To change the way that they feel inside
They begin a smile that they can no longer hide
Will you smile when you hear?
That love is so perfect love is so dear
From the love that you hear
From your eyes comes a falling tear*

I Cannot Take The Things That You Are Doing To Me

I can't take the things that you are doing to me
I think that I want to spread my wings and fly free
To search for a love that will make me feel
The love in my life that I need to live
For when we are together every day
We should feel the love for which we pray
We should express our love in what we say
And in the things that we do every day

When we can't see eye to eye
And cause each other the tears that we cry
We are not giving each other the love that we need to feel
For love is the most important thing in the lives that we live
When we hold back the words that we want to say
We are trying not to hurt each other with the words that we say
When we are not letting go of the pain that both of us can claim
Then we can't move on in the lives that we live when love calls our names

For we are afraid to open our hearts to the love that we need to feel
Because from the pain of love our hearts have never been able to heal
Baby I can't take it any more I'm close to walking out of the door
It's time that we start to give each other the love that we both need to feel
To ignite a fire in each other's hearts or from each other to finally depart
It is time for us to choose to give each other the love that we need to feel
Because the love that we feel gives us a reason to want to live
Baby I can't take it any more I'm close to walking out of the door

It is pass time that you begin to understand
What it means to have a relationship with another woman or man
It is pass time that you begin to understand
How our lives crisscross as we journey upon the land
It is time that you open your eyes to see
How the pain of love can change the hearts of you and me
The love that we give need to ignite a fire in our hearts
For the love that we share can be strengthened until the day that we depart

When You Are Looking At Me

When you are looking at me
Tell me what do you see?
Tell me how do I make you feel
Is the love that you feel imagined or real
When you are looking into my eyes
Tell me what can you recognize?
What are you afraid to see?
That you should be giving your love to me

Can't you feel the beat of my heart?
When we come together after being apart
Can't you feel the excitement in the air?
For when I see that is how much I care
When we are together, I burn with fire
For it is your love that I truly desire
I want to pull you into my embrace
And let you feel how my heartbeat race

When you are looking at me
Tell me what you see
Do you see a love that was meant to be?
When you look into the heart of me
Don't be afraid of the love that you feel
Because my love for you will always be real
For my eyes are open for you to see
That you should be giving your love to me

Sometimes in life we throw the dice
Wanting love to touch us twice
With a feeling of love that feels so nice
When we are together, we are in paradise
No matter where we may be
When it is each other that we see
Both of our heartbeats start to race
For the love that we long to embrace

You Became The Voice Of Everyone That Were Lost

You became the voice of everyone that were lost
Never knowing what would be your cost
You became a picture for everyone to see
You revealed the faces of you and me
You stood up and finally showed the world
That we could be any boy or girl
You became the face of someone that some people did not want to see
You stood up for the future of you and me

The defining moment in the lives that we live
Comes from the dream that you were able to fulfill
You have changed our lives forever more
When you opened our hearts to see you walk through that door
You have changed the lives of everyone that will live
With the dreams that you were able to fulfill
You have shown a nation that was tearing itself apart
That there can be courage and strength in every heart

Your trials and tribulation was truly great
Yet standing up for others you did not hesitate
We can all feel hope whenever we think of you
For you have showed us that we can be in control of our destinies too
Although we may never be as great as you
You have showed us that we can take pride in the things that we can do
You are an example of how dreams can come true
When we search inside our hearts to find the faith to see our lives through

Maybe you were not able to complete all of your plans
With so many complications it is easy to understand
Yet you do not need to despair
For you have touched the hearts of people everywhere
You have changed everyone's perception of how a person can be
You have opened the doors that has changed people's reality
I think that one of the problems in the lives that we live
Is that some of us have forgotten that you gave up your life so that we may live

We Cannot Be Given Everything

We cannot be given everything for later to us that won't mean a thing
For we will keep asking for more every time we see you walk through the door
It may hurt your heart to see us in need especially if we begin to plead
But every one of us needs to decide if we want to fail or if we want to succeed
You can give us the tools with which to succeed
So that we may be able to fulfill our needs
Teach us that we just cannot stand by and let others sacrifice for our needs
For we need to go out and work for our dreams to succeed

A painful lesson may be hard for us to bear
But some of us need that lesson before we truly start to care
You have done what you thought were right to shield us day and night
To many of us you have been a guiding light
 Let not your heart not despair when you think that we are there
For the lessons that you have taught us we will always care
For we must not give up in what we decide to do
And turn around and or everything depend upon you

For there are many times when we may be tempted to reach out our hands
And through your caring for us let you do whatever you can
For us to take that point of view would be for us to take advantage of you
And in so taking advantage of you means that we really never understood you
Yet as we sometimes walk by you and we see your tears
We come to understand what you went through for us through the years
How you heart were open with the love that you were able to give
How we may have sometimes taken advantage of you through the years

In ourselves we should begin to feel shame for we are the ones to blame
We should not have taken advantage of you trying to make our dreams come true
We should have looked upon your face and saw the love for us you had embraced
We should have looked upon your face and saw the tears that we could trace
We cannot be given everything for later to us it may not mean everything
But to some of us everything that you have given will mean everything
We will gladly give back to you whatever we can to make your dreams come true
For we know how precious is the heart of someone as precious as you

Before The Moment Will Disappear

Before the moment will disappear open your heart so that you can hear
For there is a song that you can feel that will make you want to live
There is a song that will come to us a song about a love that we can trust
When you open your heart, you will hear how a song can cause you to cry a tear
For you will always care when you feel love reaching out to you from everywhere
For you will feel how precious is the love that someone can give
You will not be able to stop that falling tear when such love will appear
For every year we open our hearts to hear love that can be whispered in our ear

A love that we can feel in the lives that we live
Before the moment will disappear, we can open our hearts to hear
How precious is the sound of a falling tear when it reaches our ear?
Hearing the sound of love reaching out to us with a love that we can trust
For when love enters our hearts our lives begin to change from the start
There is a feeling that we never want to stop no matter what time is on the clock
There is a feeling that takes over our hearts that we never want to stop
And our eyes will open to see the ones that came before through that open door

Bringing the love that would forever change the way that we would feel
Bringing the love that would forever change the lives that we live
For love will forever change the way that we see things
For love will open our hearts and make us want to sing
And with every whisper of love that is carried by the wind
We can feel that it is our hearts that begins to mend
With every joyful noise that can be heard from far away
It is the sound of love that seem to forever in our hearts stay

Before the moment will disappear open your heart so that you can hear
For there is a song that you can feel that will make you want to live
There is a song that will come to us a song about a love that we can trust
When you open your heart, you will hear how a song can cause you to cry a tear
For when love reaches out for you from everywhere
Then you will always know that for you someone will care
For we are all searching to feel the tenderness found in love's embrace
For we all enjoy seeing the tears running down our faces as love leaves its traces

I Live For The Hunt

*I live for the hunt and to see that next marvelous stunt
To see someone floating in the air and living the lives that they care
I live for the future that will come to be I live for other people and not just for me
I live for everything that I can ever see I live to be the best that I can ever be
I don't know what you would do if you were me
I don't know if you will open your heart and try to live your life like me
To not be afraid to let other people see
In the living of my life what it means to be the best that I can be*

*I know that there will one day come to be someone that I can see
Who will open their hearts to me with a love that is meant to be
For I live my life for the love that I will one day see
To treasure the moment when I see someone with love reaching out for me
For the love that I will feel will determine the person that I will come to be
For I want to feel a love that will set my heart and my soul free
I want to wake up to the dawn of another day
With the knowledge that I cannot in bed stay*

*With the knowledge that our lives cannot be lived that way
I get down on my knees I pray for that feeling of love that can brighten my day
I live to see how my journey will unfold as every day I grow old
For the day when I will see the love in my life that was foretold
When I will be able to walk along the beach and feel the sand beneath my feet
And to have the ones that I love and the ones that love me always within reach
To look into their eyes and be able to see such a love that will always be
That they will always have a love in their hearts for me*

*I heard it said, so many times before for love we should leave an open door
Although our bodies will continue to grow old
We will always have in our hearts the need to feel a love that can touch our soul
For it is the love and caring that we feel that helps us to want to live
Even if all of our memories are not there it will still be love that we care
I live for the hunt to see someone that will always express the love we all care
I kneel down on my knees and I pray for that feeling of love to come my way
For as I grow old in my heart, I will always want to feel that I am loved every day*

As We Live Our Lives Year By Year

As we live our lives from year to year there will be times when we cry our tears
For the memories within our minds can come back to us at any time
Memories of the way we used to feel as we recall the lives that we used to live
Memories of a time long passed return to our lives at last
For we find happiness and pain as we live our lives year by year
For there are times when we give into our fears
And in a moment of weakness, we cry our tears
As we recall life's ups and downs through the years
In a moment of weakness our tears may fall
For deep within our hearts, we know that on God we can always call
For when our emotions start to become too strong
Within our hearts we never want to forget what is right or wrong
We never want to lash out at someone nearby
Just to see the tears that they may cry
For the way other people feel we should learn to respect
Before we are the ones that are being shown such neglect

When it comes to our feelings, we want other people to show respect
Then how can we turnaround and show other people disrespect
For to hurt someone out of neglect will create in us such feelings of regret
For when it comes to love who can say what conditions will always be met
As we live our lives from year to year the way that we feel is not always clear
For there are events in our lives that changes our hearts from day to day
From a second to a minute and from a minute to an hour
We want to feel a love that can lift us from the bottom floor to the highest tower
We should be thankful for the words of love that we are able to hear
We should be thankful for the love that can bring out in us a tear
We should be thankful that we are given another day to be able to feel
How precious can be the love in the lives that we live
As we live our lives from year to year there will be time when we cry our tears
For the memories in our minds can come back at any time
Memories of the way we used to feel as we recall the lives that we used to live
Should always bring a face to our faces for the love that we were able to embrace

I Have Been With You For Such A Long Time

I've been with you for such a long time
Yet you don't know that your love still lives in my heart and mind
For although we may argue fuss and fight
We know that after time has passed everything will be alright
We come back together to share the love that we feel
For we can't deny each other the love that we need to live
We burn with a desire for a love that we want to feel
Yet because of our pride we hold back the love that we can give

With the love that we feel in the lives that we live
We are given the moments that we can treasure that is beyond measure
There are times when we hurt each other because of our pride
But the love in our hearts gives us a chance to stay by each other's side
For when we have been together for such a long time
How can we separate the love from our hearts and our minds
When we try to deny the love that we feel
It comes back to us in the pain that love gives

Leaving us with the tears that we cry
It is too late for us to tell each other good-by
We cannot turn away from the love that we feel
For we need each other in the lives that we live
I know that there are people out there that feel the same way that we do
When they go to sleep at night, they call out each other's names like me
and you For the love that we feel will always live in our hearts
Keeping us together when our lives get hard

When we see other people drift apart
We remember the love that lives in our hearts
We remember how we used to argue, fuss and fight
And cry ourselves to sleep until late in the night
With the love that lives in our hearts and our minds
We were able to forgive each other over the passage of time
For the pain of love can give us such regret
When the love that we truly feel we try to neglect

Here Is To Me and Here Is To You

Here is to you and to me and what people are able to see
For when you are cold, I'm hot and when I'm hot you are not
For when we are burning with sizzling heat
How can we ever come together to meet
For when we are burning with the anger that we feel
It can take a long time before our hearts will begin to heal
For we turn away from the love in our hearts
Thinking that from each other we should depart

In our anger there are words we say
That continues to live in our hearts everyday
For when we are both burning with heat
It is with each other that we complete
For instead of coming together in the middle
We both pick up the ball and double dribble
For we both begin to break the rules
Not wanting to be the first one to be used

With no love being shared between us
We slowly begin to lose each other's trust
We are going down a road that we do not want to go
But sometimes it is hard for us to tell ourselves no
A road that will leave us with a pain that we will come to know
For it is our pride that we continue to let show
For there are times when we lose our way
When we will listen to what other people will say

For we forget that not everyone wants to see our lives work out
For there are some people that will feel joy when we scream and shout
For we cry out in our hearts that we need each other in the lives that we live
And then we begin to wonder why did we let other people tell us how we feel
We are letting our pride push our love aside and deepening the pain in our hearts
From each other drifting apart instead of forgiving each other from the start
Here is to me and you and the changes that life will put us through

No More Tears Will I Cry

No more tears will I cry
I will raise my head to the pie in the sky
I will accept what will come to be
I will accept the destiny given to me
No more tears will I cry
For being afraid to give life a try
For I can now share the way that I feel
For I am no longer afraid to help someone's heart to heal

No more will I just stand by
And watch the tears that someone cry
I will try to help and heal their pain
Even if they will not call out my name
No more will I close my eyes to what I see
And give into the fear that is inside of me
I will never again turn away from the love that I can give
When I know that my love can help someone's heart begin to heal

No more will I deny the love that I can share
For people need to know that someone care
Someone that can give them a glimmer of hope
To lighten their hearts so they are able to laugh and joke
No more will I deny the future that can be
For I can accept the changes in me
The need to share the love that lives in my heart
When I see people lives being torn apart

No more tears will I cry
No more dreams will I let die
When I have the love that I can give
That can help someone to cherish the life that they live
For in my heart I can understand when there is no love that they can feel
When there is no one around with the love that they can give
I know the pain that life can give when there is no love that we can feel
For there is a feeling of loneliness that seems to slowly drain our will

There are no more tears that we need to cry
For we know the ones we love will not just stand by and let our dreams die
They will come to us and never pass us by

They will forever wipe the tears from our eyes
They will help us to spread our wings and fly
They will help us to believe in our dreams until the day that we die
No more tears will I cry
For I will never let the love in my heart die

For I can feel the love in my heart
That will always be reaching out for me until the day that I depart
No more tears will I cry for the dreams that I let die
For the rest of my years, I will no longer give into my fears
For I will have a feeling of love that I can treasure as each moment I measure
For I know now that there will always be a feeling of love deep within my heart
No more will I deny the love that I can share
For we all need to feel that we are loved and we are cared

When Love Is More Than A Dream

When you are looking at me you think that something is wrong
For there is a feeling of love that you feel so strong
Looking into your eyes there is a love that I can see
You can't turn away from what your heart is saying about me
When there is a feeling of love that is felt so strong
How can the love that you feel ever be wrong
The intensity of the moment will not let your heart go
For as each moment passes the love in your heart continue to grow

Who can say that your feeling of love is right or wrong?
With the love that you feel the beating of your heart is ever so strong
You cannot turnaround and continue to walk away
When there are so many words in your heart that you want to say
You want to talk about the love that you are now able to feel
You want to talk about this moment in the life that you live
It is not just the imagination of your mind
It is a feeling of love that you have been searching to find

You are walking around as if you are floating in the air
You can feel your heart bursting with such love and care
You are unable to control the way that you feel
A love that you thought could never become real
With your heart filled with so much emotion
There can be no greater feeling when it comes to love's devotion
Yet you have not been able to confirm what you pray to be true
That the ones that you love feel the same way that you do

That confirmation to you will mean so much
For every part of your soul will be forever touched
For you can hear the beating of your heart
Praying that love will not end before it will start
As you look into the eyes of someone coming near
You can see a reflection of love on a face without fear
You no longer have to wonder if love is right or wrong
For there is a feeling of love reaching back to you that ever so strong

Moving In Slow Motion

When everything seems to be moving in slow motion
Take a step back in time to strengthen your devotion
Back to the memories within your mind
That has been waiting there for you to find
It is time to take a second look on the road that you took
Maybe you can look back on what you once wrote in a book
For when you get that feeling that something is wrong
You need to find the memories that can help you to grow strong

For when shadows start playing tricks on you
You can begin to doubt the things that you can do
Reflecting back on the memories that are within your mind
You can be taken back to this point in time
When you may have cried your tears of pain
But after that had fun playing in the rain
Realizing that there will always be a changing of the weather
But the ones that you love can still have a wonderful time together

There are many memories within your mind
That can become an anchor for you over the passage of time
There are memories that have been waiting to reach out to you
That can help you to understand the changes you are going through
Memories of someone just holding your hands
Giving you a comfort that you can understand
There are memories of someone drying your tears
Telling you that they will always love you throughout the years

When everything seems to be moving in slow motion
Take a step back in time to strengthen your devotion
Back to the memories within your mind
That has been waiting there for you to find
It is time to take a second look on the road that you took
Maybe you can look back on what you once wrote in a book
For when you get that feeling that something is wrong
You need to find the memories that help you to grow strong

What Is It Going To Be

Baby what is it going to be ?
What more do you need to see?
When I entered the room ?
Did I come to you too soon?
There are so many girls in the world
That I could choose to be my girl
There are so many girls in the world
That understand the meaning of a diamond or pearl

Diamonds and pearls don't have to mean money or gold
But can be an expression of a love that reaches into your soul
For love means more than diamonds and pearls
For love people will travel around the world
For all our money can suddenly disappear
And in our lifetime never again reappear
But the feeling of love that has reached into our souls
Will live in our hearts every day that we grow old

What is it going to be?
Will it be only the money that you see?
When I entered the room
Did I come to you too soon?
I may be poor when I enter your door
But there will never be another man that will love you more
For I would travel around the world
Just to make you my girl

What is it going to be?
The love of money or the love of me
What is it going to be?
The love of money or living in harmony
It is a time for you to choose
If you are ready to win or lose
It is time for you to express your true emotions
To strengthen the bonds of love's true devotions

Maybe You Think Love Has Grown Strong

Maybe you think that our love has grown strong
I'm here to tell you that something is going wrong
Can't you see that the love you are holding back
Is causing our love to begin to crack
If you are not giving me all of your heart
Then maybe from one another we should depart
For there is really no guarantee that I am able to see
That your heart truly belongs to me

When I can see the differences in the love that you give
I can begin to understand how love can change the way that you feel
For within my heart there is the stirring of doubts
From within my heart I feel to scream and shout
How can we continue to live this way?
How can we continue to love each other every day?
For when love is not truly being given from our hearts
Sooner or later from each other we will depart

When there is no understanding of your true emotions
You can be left swimming in the ocean
Unable to give the one that you are with your true devotions
You can leave the one that love you with a feeling of mixed emotions
Maybe you think that the love between us is strong
Maybe it is time to consider that you may be wrong
It is time that you come to understand your true emotions
So that the love that you give may reflect love's true devotion

When you are unable to release your true feelings inside
You are caught up in a circle of emotions that you are trying to hide
Sooner or later the feelings that you hide will be released
Until that time the worrying within your heart will never cease
You will always get caught up in lies and half-truths
Sooner or later your emotions will get the best of you
Before it is too late you should no longer hesitate
For the love in your heart will always define the road that you take

When Love May Not Be Real

I thought that our love was strong but it turned out that I was wrong
I thought you knew what was right that you opened your eyes to the light
You thought to keep me blind to the love that lived in your heart and mind
But now I see that the love in your heart was never mine
When you took me down a road that only increased the weight of my load
You wanted me to believe every word that I was told
When I held you close it was not me that you wanted the most
You took away my pride as my love for you kept me by your side

I never thought that love could turn out that way to leave me with nothing to say
I thought that your love for me would blossom one day
I thought to wake up with someone by my side
Someone whose love would give me pride
For there is so much pain that I feel in the life that I live
I know that is not the way that love should make someone feel
I can see now that my eyes were not open to see
That love can sometimes change the persons that we will come to be

We wonder why this can sometimes happen to you and me
As we reflect upon the way that our lives came to be
When love is what we are searching to feel
We have to wonder what kind of life we are willing to live
Are we willing to let go of the love that we feel in our hearts
To give up on our dreams before they start
There were mistakes that were made along the way
But I thought that love would make up for that some day

When there are so many words that are forever spoken
Leaving you with the feeling that love is still just a token
It can begin to get harder to believe the one that you love
You begin to slowly let go of the love that you dream of
To never know how true love can feel
That can be the greatest regrets in the lives that we live
Sometimes it is best that we let love go regardless if our hearts say no
We all deserve to feel a love that can help us to achieve the dreams we dream of

A Promise Made To You

I made a promise to you
A promise that is so very hard to keep
For there were changes in me
Changes that I could not foresee
I promised that I would love you every day
And from you I would never turn away
But with everything that we have been going through
I find it hard to keep the promises that I once made to you

I thought that no matter what you put me through
That I would still be able to keep my promise to you
But there were many things that you began to do
That started changing my love for you
Although you have broken your promises to me
I have never broken my promises to you.
For love to me was never a game
To be thrown away in search of money and fame

To break someone's heart and leave them crying in the dark
Can destroy the love that lives in their hearts
Changing them forever more
Leaving them afraid to let love enter their door
For there are times when love can tear us apart
To leave us crying our tears from a broken heart
But still I have kept my promises to you
Regardless of what you have put me through

I can see that lately there have been changes in me
Changes in my heart that I was unable to foresee
There have been changes in our hearts
And from each other we have been drifting apart
Maybe my love for you have faded away
Because I find that today is a different day
Maybe I am tired of listening to what you have to say
Maybe broken promises slowly took away my love for you every day

Watching You For Some Time

I have been watching you for some time
You may think that it is no business of mine
It is cold outside and you are welcome to come in
I know that right now you may need a friend
I know that you may feel lost and alone
That within your heart you are trying to be strong
But there are times when you need a helping hand
When you need someone that can help you understand

I may be just one man but I am offering you a helping hand
Especially if you feel that your life is not going as planned
I don't care if you are young or you are old
I just want to help to warm you when you are feeling cold
I am not asking for anything in return
It is just that for you I am able to show concern
There is nothing for me that you need to do
I just want you to know that someone cares about you

For in the lives that we live and the many ways that we feel
There should always be someone with love to give
Even when we may not know each other
That does not mean that we should not care about one another
We are surely sisters and brothers
As well as someone's fathers and mothers
when it comes to the lives that we live
We should care about the way that each other feel

I know that people may say that I am not smart but I do not care
For I know that in my heart for other people I will always care
That every life to me will always be precious and rare
With their own memories, their hopes and dreams beyond compare
Trying to find a reason to live and love that they can feel
That is why I open my heart with the love that I can give
I may be just one man but when it comes to that feeling of love
I know that in everyone's heart that is what all people are dreaming of

I Cannot Take The Things That You Are Doing To Me

Baby I can't take the things that you are doing to me
I think that I want to spread my wings and fly free
To search for a love that will make me feel
That I am loved in the life that I live
For when we are together every day
We should be able to feel the love for which we pray
We should express our love with the words we say
And in the things that we do every day

When we can't see eye to eye and we cause each other the tears that we cry
We are not giving each other the love that brings tears to our eyes
We need to feel every day that we are loved in each other's hearts
For that will allow us to stay together instead of drift apart
For when we are holding back the words that we need to say
We are placing obstacles in our hearts and minds everyday
We are creating such a pain in each other's hearts
That we are slowly creating a rift that could tear our lives apart

Letting go of the pain that we may be able to claim
We can begin to realize that we both bear part of the blame
Losing ourselves in the search for money and fame
We may slowly begin to disrespect each other's names
We may be thinking that we cannot take it anymore
We may be close to walking out the door
It is time that we re-ignite a fire in each other's hearts
To give each other a love that can stop us from drifting apart

It is time that we put to rest our feelings of doubt
That we take the time to work our problems out
It is time that we put to rest our feelings of doubt
It is time that we let the love in our hearts come pouring out
It is time that we reconcile the way that we feel
And finally come to an understanding of the love that we need to give
For that will prevent each of us from wanting to spread our wings and fly free
It will bring back a love that will forever live in the hearts of you and me

I Can See Inside of You

I can see things that you are going through
I can feel my heart going out to you
It's not the fancy clothes that you wear
It is not the money or the jewelry that I care
It is the moments that we are together from the start
It is the love that we can share that can brighten our hearts
It is the words that you say and how you kneel down and pray
That our love for each other will grow stronger every day

It's the love that I can feel coming from a heart that is real
It is the love that you give that has the power to change how I feel
For in your eyes I can see the way that you are reaching out for me
Giving me a promise that the love in our heart for me will always be
It is not the clothes that you wear or the jewelry that I care
It's the way that you make me feel when I know for me you will always be there
With the love that you give I can feel at peace in the life that I live
For there is an understanding of the love that we are willing to give

You can wear a diamond ring and have the perfect voice to sing
But without the love coming from your heart it will not mean anything
For you will be an empty vessel from the start without the love in your heart
With only to live your life waiting for the time that you will depart
I can see the inside of you which opens my heart to the love I feel for you
I can see the best part of you as the love in your heart come shining through
For through your eyes I can see that you have been reaching out for me
Within my heart I know that is the way that true love should be

Sharing a love that is meant to be can leave us with a feeling of being free
For there will always be a feeling of excitement in the hearts of you and me
It is in these moments that we are finally able to see
How we are able to strengthen the love in the hearts of you and me
It is in the love that we can share that will brighten our hearts
That will give us the peace that we need to feel from the start
It is not in the diamonds and pearls money or fame
It is in the love we give that helps us to treasure the moments in the lives we live

Our Love Is Worth Defending

Here we go again and again
Turning around and defending a love we never want to end
A love that had a strange beginning
That turned into a love that we want to be never-ending
Refusing to put each other down
Even when family and friends come around
For we knew that our lives could be turned upside down
Knowing that we could put our lives on a merry-go-round

If we were to turn around and talk about each other
We know that our families and friends would separate us one from another
Affecting the trust that we give to each other
And the love that we feel for one another
Our smiles can be turned into frowns when our families and friends come around
For we know that if we put each other down we put our lives on a merry-go-round
We have learned from one another we should have more concern for each other
For no matter how long we are together precious moments can last forever

It can be a crying shame the way people talk about each other's names
Allowing their families and their friends to sometimes turn their love into a game
Sometimes becoming jealous of the closeness that we can feel
Our families and friends can break us apart because of the jealousies of the heart
Instead of wishing the best for us
They are sometimes the ones that break down our trust
They should be the ones that are there to support us
To help us to strengthen a relationship that we can trust

When it is our families and our friends that we choose
When it comes to our love for one another we will lose
When we want our love for each other to be never ending
Then we should know that our love for each other will always be worth defending
For even through the hardships that we will go through
Families and friends can sometimes turn away from me and you
But if we are able to hold on to a love that we know is true
Then there will come a day when our dreams will come true

Can You Tell Me Why

Can you tell me why
So many of our children end up behind bars
Can you tell me why
So many of our children no longer make a wish on a shooting star
For our children are caught up in the world that they are living in
Never knowing when or how their lives will come to an end
Trying to fit in with their families and friends
They can sometimes lose sight of themselves in the end

Driving fast cars and sleeping late into the night
They are too tired to wake up in the early morning light
When we try and tell them that time is passing them by
They leave us with the tears that we sometimes cry
For they are our children and we love them so much
But with them it seems that we are sometimes losing touch
When all that we want to do is to help make their dreams come true
To give them a better life and to help them to live with any pain or sacrifice

There are times when we ask them to sit and talk
To maybe take the time to go with us for a walk
But sometimes they turn around and say maybe another day
Leaving us to say that will be okay
We try to show them how much we care
But how can we show them when they are sometimes not there
For when they are out in the streets
We worry about our children and the people they meet

For in the world that we are living in
We don't know when or how our lives will come to an end
So we sit down and worry about the lives that our children will live
For love in our hearts for our children is what we will always feel
For we want our children to feel the love that we can give
We want to create the moments they can treasure everyday they live
Can you tell me why so many of our children end up behind bars
For when we look upon our children they are the shining stars

It is okay for them to drive fancy cars
But they should never forget who they really are
They should never forget that their lives are rare

And that no matter what happens to them we will always care
For no matter how their lives turn out to be
They will always be a part of you and me
And when they feel that life is sometimes unfair
We want them to know that for them we will be there

Although there are times when we are not there
We want them to always feel how much we care
There will be times when their eyes will be open to see
That we cannot always be where we want to be
We pray that at those moments they are able to forgive us
With an understanding that with us they can place their trust
Whatever their decisions will come to be
Their lives will always be precious to you and me

For in the world that we are living in
We don't know when or how our lives will come to an end
We are only here for a moment in time
To share the love that lives in our hearts and minds
To try and give our children a better life to live
For that is the way that all fathers and mothers should feel
For in the world that we are living in
In ourselves and in our children is where true change can begin

There Will Come A Day

There will come a day
When to the world I have so much to say
When my voice will ring out loud and clear
You don't have to be afraid of the words you hear
For the words that I have to say
May change the way that you feel today
You can open your heart to dream
You can change what your life will come to mean

For one day you will be able to hear
How beautiful are the voices of the Angels that are always near
For their voices will ring out loud and clear
Open your heart to the love that God can give
You see I was born with a dream in my heart
To be free to share my love from the start
To be able to open everyone's eyes to see
How the wonder of God's love can truly be.

For when you look into my eyes I want you to realize
The reflection of what you see comes from the love God gives to me
A love that helps me to overcome my pain and sacrifice
A love that I can accept without having to think twice
For I know that I will never be alone
When in God's kingdom I will have a home
For God has given his blessings to me
With the knowledge of what will come to be

I will never again be afraid to raise my voice loud and clear
For I know that the words that I say can help to ease your fear
You see I am only human like you
I sometimes lose control in the things that I do
In those times I kneel down and pray
Please! God take this anger away!
Give me the strength to be kind in the words that I say
Forgive me when I sometimes do things the wrong way

For I know that your forgiveness can help me to grow strong
I know that in my heart you will never leave me standing alone
That is why I say when you hear voices do not have a fear
For they could be the voices of God's Angels whispering in your ear

So that when you open your heart you will also be able to feel
How God's love can also change the life that you live
For the Angels of God will always be near
Waiting for you to allow them to ease your fear

I was once afraid to raise my voice loud and clear
But now I want to voice out loud so that people may hear
That God loves all of us so very dear
For if that was not true then we would not be here
We would not be here to touch each other's lives
To give each other the love that could forever survive
Through each other's love we can all grow strong
For we know that in God's kingdom we will one day find a home

There is a sound that I Sometimes hear

Sometimes it is hard to tell if the sound is far or near
For it is just the beginning of a whisper that I hear
A whisper about someone that I knew before
Someone who was able to open for me another door
A door that could reach across time and space
To reach out and touch my soul from any place
Leaving a memory in my heart that never seems to depart
A call that was so great that with an answer I could never hesitate

I let that memory reach inside of my soul
To excite my heart every day that I will grow old
I let my heart begin to believe what that memory could truly mean
That life have so much meaning when there was a feeling of love worth dreaming
For holding on to that whisper has truly changed my life
It helped me to understand why I go through so much pain and sacrifice
For a whisper helped me to reconcile my sins
So that I may enter into God's kingdom in the end

It is a whisper that we can sometimes understand
When we are faced with so much sacrifice as we live upon the land
It is a whisper that we would pray would come be
That through God's love we would one day see
When we are wondering what is going on in our lives
When we are searching for the strength to survive
It will be that whisper that will come to mean so much
A whisper for which every soul will one day be touched

Imagine someone willing to sacrifice everything for you
Willing to give up their dreams so you may understand what their love means
A whisper of a love so true there will be an opening of the hearts of me and you
For we will be changed with the words we say and the things we do
A sound that could reach across time and space
To reach out and touch my soul from any place
Leaving a memory in my heart that never seems to depart
A call that was so great that with an answer I could never hesitate

I Have Traveled Near And Far

*I have traveled near and far
Sometimes I had to walk instead of ride in a car
There were places that I was able to see
That touched the very heart of me
For there were people that I were able to see
That changed how my future would come to be
For whether we are young or we are old
Each one of us had a story to be told*

*For People could see it upon our faces
How our life's journey has left its traces
For we cannot hide the things that we had to go through to stay alive
We cannot deny the things that we had to do just to survive
We may be young or we may be old
We are still so much love within our souls
I have traveled far and near
And in many places left a tear*

*But to see the way that we treat each other
Can make me wonder about our love for one another
But there are also the days when the best in us will came out
And we show each other what caring for each other is all about
A validation of the world that I live in
Show me that the love in our hearts will never end
For even in the dark moments of our lives
There will always be someone that makes us feel grateful we are alive*

*Someone that we may see far or near
Someone that we may see year after year
Someone that will forever cause us a tear
For the memories they leave in our hearts year after year
A validation of the love that we are able to always dream of
A validation of what we seek when we close our eyes to sleep
A validation of our willing to forgive the mistakes that we make
As we meet each other along the roads that we take*

I Wake Up To The Sound Of A Voice

I wake up to the sound of a voice
Saying wake up it is time to rejoice
For the time is at hand
It is the fulfillment of God's plan
My eyes begin to open but it is hard to see
For the sleepiness of the night has not left me
As I become fully awake there is a sudden breath that I take.
For the beauty of the sight bathe me with such a wonderful light

For I could hardly believe what my heart truly perceived.
With so many Angels floating in the air
It seemed like they were floating everywhere
Calling out to me to accept God's mystery
Time for me to look upon life's history
Everything around me became so bright
That I was blinded by the beauty of the light
As my eyes became crystal clear with such a wondrous sight

For my time was at hand
With the knowledge that I was a part of God's plan
I was in a dream come true
A promise that has been waiting for me and you
For God's love was given to me
With everything that I was able to see
There was no fear inside of my heart
For I had been waiting for the time that I would depart

Our lives are judged by what we say and do
Even in our dreams we stand trial too
For we try to interpret what we go through doing the day
To only wake up in the morning with the meaning slipped away
I wake up to the sound of a voice
Saying wake up it is time to rejoice
For the time is at hand
This is a fulfillment of God's plan

Remember Me

Remember me when you enter into the heavens above
Shine down on me with your gift of love
Remember me when I cry my tears
For I will remember you throughout my years
Remember me when I once was a child
How when I heard your name I had such beautiful smile
For the memories of your love is what I will always dream of
Praying that you have entered the heavens above

You gave me a reason to live with the love that you could give
You were always a blessing in the life that I lived
You brought tears to my eyes for the dreams that you made me realize
You taught me that even with pain and sacrifice love could survive
Remember me when your father you will see
For with you and your father is where I want to be
To be embraced in the love that I can feel
There is nothing in this world that I would not give

Remember me when I close my eyes to sleep
For you caused my tears to weep
For I was a child born upon the earth
A child that needed your love since the day of my birth
Remember me with the love that you give
For you made my life so wonderful to live
For with my belief in you I try to be a reflection of you with the things that I do
For you made me believe that dreams could really come true

I may fall short of what you desire but for you I would go into a burning fire
Knowing that in your heart you want me to receive what I truly desire
Remember me for it is your name that lives in my heart
For I have never give up on you from the start
Wherever my life will take me I know that one day it will be you that I see
For I know that wherever you are you are watching over me
For at the end of the day when I kneel down and pray
I pray for the blessing I received when you passed my way

It will be your voice that I hear telling me to cast away my fear
That no matter where I am you will always be near
To keep my love strong in my heart
For you will be there to guide me into the light when I depart

Remember me for I will always remember you
For you taught me how love could make dreams come true
Remember me when you are in the heavens above
Shine down on me with your gift of love

Remember me when you enter into the heavens above
Shine down on me with your gift of love
Remember me when I cry my tears
For I will remember you throughout my years
Remember me when I once was a child
How when I heard your name I had such beautiful smile
For the memories of your love is what I will always dream of
Praying that you have entered the heavens above

When Life Takes Us Down A Bumpy Road

When life takes us down a bumpy road
We have to learn how to balance our load
As we remember what we once was told
That life can make us become very old
For the problems in our minds
Can cause us to worry all the time
For with every sleepless night
We are unwilling to wake up to the morning light

For our lives can change at a moment notice
Like the coming of the flying locust
Although we may begin to despair
When we think that we are not being treated fair
There is a feeling of hope that is always there
Hope that has only been lost somewhere
For when we are moving down a road too fast
It can seem like the moments will forever last

We was once told that life could make become very old
When we allow our problems to take control of our souls
When we give into our fears it can be hard for our hearts to heal
As our eyes become wet from the crying of our tears
When we open our hearts we take a chance in the lives we live
For we can never want to turn away from the love that we seek to feel
For when we kneel down and pray God can open our eyes to find a better way
God can give us the strength to reconcile the way that we feel every day

When our lives goes down a bumpy road
God hears our prayers and gives us the strength to bear our load
Even when we begin to despair God will always be there
For God wants us to feel his love and care
Giving us the strength that we need to feel
With God's love in our hearts we will successful in the lives we live
Going down a bumpy road when it is hard to bear our load
Can strengthen our will when we change the way that we feel

Looking Up At The Mountaintop

Looking up at the mountaintop I can feel my heart begin to drop
For every step that I take seem to be so hard to make
Yet I know that I cannot stop even if to the ground I will drop
For I have been told that it is too far like reaching for a distant star
For I have been told that it is too far that I need a car
To accept what they say mean they can control my way
Defining the things that I can do because that is what they want to be true
They try to limit my mind telling me that I am wasting my time

That I should accept what I see and let that come to be
Truly their eyes are blind to see for they do not know me
For they do not understand what my life will mean
If I listen to what they say and give up my dreams
They can let the mountaintop cause their hearts to drop
But I will not stop until I have reached the mountaintop
No one can ever say the things that I will or will not do
For they have not experienced the things that I have went through

That is for me to decide for I have God on my side
I do not say this because of my pride but because of the love that I feel inside
God will guide my way no matter what anyone will say
God will give me the strength to reach the star if I decide to go that far.
I hold on to the faith that I have in my heart
For God's love sets each of us apart
As we discover what God's love means to our hearts
If we need to reach the mountaintop God will give us the strength to never stop

Whatever my goals in life will be
I know that God will always be watching over me
There is no one that can place a limit on the things that I can do
For within my heart I know that God will give me the strength to see it through
Looking up at the mountaintop I can feel my heart begin to drop
For every step that I take seem to be so hard to make
Yet with a smile upon my face and a love that I can trace
It is the beauty of the life that I live that I will forever embrace

What We Can And Cannot Achieve

When people try and tell us what we can and cannot achieve
Then they are trying to tell us what we dare to dream
For when they look at us they simply cannot see
That they have no control of what we decide we want to be
They look at us through eyes that are old
They are not strong enough to look deeply into our souls
For they cannot see beyond their own pride
When they judge us by what they decide

To look upon someone and say that they know what is true
Then they see a reflection of themselves and not a reflection of me or you
We can only pray that the time will come when they will understand
That they have no right to judge another woman or man
For only God can judge every child, woman and man
For God knows each of our destinies when we are born upon this land
With human emotions and predetermined ideas
Prejudice and mistrust will continue to live

Looking at a person and the clothes they wear
Cannot truly determine the load that they will bear
When we cannot walk in their shoes
We will not know the reasons behind the choices they choose
How can in our hearts we truly believe
That we can tell each other what we can truly achieve
For each of us were born to be different at our births
To choose the paths that we will walk upon the earth

We need to take a deeper look inside of our souls
Before the love in our hearts begins to turn cold
For through our actions we need to show each other compassion
For the things that we do in the lives that we live can create a chain reaction
We need to look upon the people that we see
We need to determine that they are just like you and me
We need to find the love in our hearts
That can bring us together instead of separating us from the start

Imagination And Me

Imagination and me as far as the eyes can see
The flowers and the trees and the feeling of a gentle breeze
There is a beauty that is calling out to me
With the colors of the rainbow that I am able to see
Defining how th moment can truly come to be
The falling of the rain returning back to the sea
For every rain drop bears its own name
Just like the birds in the trees causing the rustling of the leaves

The sound of the wind and the cycle that will never end
I close my eyes and pretend that I am surrounded by family and friends
I pray that they will always be with me until my journey comes to an end
For there are so many precious memories that can come from families and friends
with the sound of children at play that always seem to brighten my day
For they cast their light of love back into the heavens above
As I look around me there is so much beauty that I see
That I open my heart to release the love inside of me

With an understanding of why I am here from my eye falls a tear
A tear for a love that can forever be coming from the inside of the heart of me
A love that I can forever share to change the hearts of people everywhere
A love that people will forever feel regardless of the lives that they live
Imagination and me a reflection of my destiny
As far as the eyes can see love can change what will come to be
For love is like an burning ember to a fire
It fans the flames of the emotions that we desire

Imagination and me as far as the eyes can see
The flowers and the trees and the feeling of a gentle breeze
There is a beauty calling out to me
With the colors of the rainbow that I am able to see
The closing of my eyes for the wonder that I realize
For the reality and the dreams that I am able to visualize
Imagination and me bringing out the beauty that I can be
Awakening my heart to the blessings that gives me peace when I am resting

The Flowers Of Our Lives Struggle To Survive

The flowers of our lives struggle to survive
Needing to be cared for with love to stay alive
Looking to the ones who came before to open for them another door
For the strength of their love is needed more and more
To the love that they need to feel they can never say no
Especially when they first begin to learn and grow
They need to be cared for in the day and in the night
They need to be made to feel that everything will be alright

To be given comfort so that they may thrive in the dark or light
They are the flowers that need to grow in the brightest of light
The flowers of our lives can grow strong when listening to the beauty of songs
For the music excited the heart when it begins from the start
The music that excites the inner spirits with such joy and happiness
A happiness that we would never want our children to miss
To grow and prosper in so many ways that is what we will always pray
For the flowers of our lives brightens our lives every day

The flowers of our lives blossoming in the day or in the night
The flowers of our lives being guided to do what is right
If we take the time to listen for awhile
The flowers of our lives will always feel to smile
When we shelter them from the pouring of the rain
We seek to shelter them from sacrifice and pain
Our love for them we will forever feel
For we brought them into this world to live

The flowers of our lives are the reason we are here
For with each passing moment we watch over them year by year
Someday the flower of their lives will appear
And we will watch over them until it is time for us to dis-appear
until it is time for our lives to come to an end
We will show them how the love in their hearts can begin
We will show them through our love and our careEven when there are times for them we may not be there

I Pray That It Is Not Too Late

I pray that it is not too late
To change the road that I need to take
I pray that it is not too late to seek forgiveness from you
For all the things that I put you through
I pray that it is not too late to feel the love that you can give
I'm sorry for the pain that I made you feel
I'm sorry that I cause you fear and doubt
As to what my love for you was all about

For such a long time we have been hurting inside
Because we have been holding on to our foolish pride
Neither one of us wanting to be the first one to give in
But wanting this cycle of pain and anger to come to an end
In my heart I know that I still love you
Regardless of what we are going through
For I can see the tears that you try to hide
I can see the words that you hold back because of your pride

The changing of the words that we say
Can come from us beginning to listen to each other every day
Sometimes our pride can take us for a ride
Leaving us alone with no one by our side
Leaving us with a pain that we can forever feel
Making it hard for us to change the way that we live
Let me be the first to tell you how I feel
I will love you every day that I shall live

It is time that we forget our foolish pride
It is time that we let the love in our hearts decide
Too much time has passed us by when we turned away
When we should have been listening to each other every day
We are being given another chance to change the lives that we live
Do we really want to cast aside the love that we still feel
I pray that it is not too late
For us to change the road that we need to take

When I Count To Three I know Where You Will Be

When I count to three I know where you will be
Remember me when we are apart and the love deep within your heart
When you open your eyes to see remember the child that I used to be
How you and I climbed up a tree the way that you looked up and smiled at me
Through the life that I had to live remember the love that I was able to give
Remember the way that you would feel when I was there to dry your tears
When I told you to always stay real you changed the way that you did feel
When I count to three I know where you will be

I can remember the pain when you hurt your knee
How you looked up with those pretty eyes at me
I wished that I could have eased your pain
To bring back that smile that you had always claimed
One two three you were the prettiest girl that I ever did see
One two three remember you and me
The good times that we had and when we made each other sad
One two three together you and me

We were going to change everything that we did see
We thought the world would revolve around you and me
When we found that diamond or pearl we were going to go around the world
We were young and we were strong
Ready to go out and change what went wrong
One two three my girl is now with me
For when I count to three you are now here with me
Looking up at me with the prettiest eyes I ever did see

Sharing the good times and the bad times
Sharing the happy times and the sad times
We gave each other hope when as children we played jump rope
We made each other cry when we told each other good-by
We then turned around and smiled for it was just a lie
For our love will endure until the day that we die
Remember me when we are apart and the love deep within your heart
For I have always loved you from deep down in my heart

I Never Thought You Could Be Interested In A Man Like Me

I never thought that you could be interested in a man like me
I thought that you were interested in the young guys that you see
You will never be older than me that much I can guarantee
For time will pass the same for you and me
I see a young girl footloose and fancy free
Running around and looking at all that she can see
With wonderful thoughts of love spinning around in her mind
For in the living of her life she has plenty of time

Catching the eyes of every young guy that passes her by
Some of them come back around just to tell her hi
Yes, a wonderful sight you are to see even to one as old as me
To be young again and experience the beauty of life
Even if there will also be pain and sacrifice
A fanciful thought that we old men sometimes think
Oh! How our hearts can jump with joy at the ideal of feeling that first kiss
Of that first girl who touched our hearts so dear that we may still miss

For love is what we feel when our lives first begin
Love will be what we want to feel when our lives come to an end
For you to be so interested in me to take the time to talk with me
When I pass you by it can sometimes bring a tear to my eyes
For life's little surprises can give an old man like me a reason to want to live knowing that love in my heart is what I can still feel
You shine a light that I am able to see
Filling my heart with a happiness that reaches deep inside of me

When everything seems dark I can remember your face
For there are memories of you that I can trace
For maybe at this moment in our lives we were drawn together
For there are moments that can live in someone's heart forever
To share the way that we feel so that we could treasure the lives that we live
For young or old we needed to listen and hear each other's story to be told.
Love can bloom between the young and the old
When there is a connection that exists between two souls

Sometimes love mean having to say good-by

Sometimes love means having to say good-by
Even if it will brings out the tears that we sometimes cry
For when it is each other that we always seem to blame
Into each other lives we bring sorrow and pain
Although it may be hard to accept what we come to know
There comes a time when we should let each other go
For when we are caught up in the blaming game
Into each other's lives we bring sorrow and shame

We may not always understand the words that each other say
For our words can get twisted and come out in a different way
For we can be hurting each other without an understanding
That can adversely affect the lives that we are planning
We have to slowly begin to change how we feel
If we truly want to stay together in the lives that we live
We know how slowly time can pass
When we are faced with the seeds of doubts that was planted in the past

For each time when there is a moment of blame
It takes away from the love that we want to claim
For the slow death of the love in our hearts
Can sometimes tear our hearts apart
With our feelings of passion slowly disappearing
We are left with our feelings of doubts that keep reappearing
We are left with the words that we do not say
For fear the words will be taken the wrong way

The foundation of our love will continue to be shaken
For each moment of passion that has been forsaken
For our voices can sometimes become silent
As we think about having to become self-reliant
For it can all start with the blame game
As we cause each other to feel sorrow and pain
It would be wise of us to tell each other how we feel
So that we can clear our minds and let our hearts begin to heal

Although I May Wish For Younger Days

Although I may wish for younger days
I know that time has already slipped away
For the moments could never last
For each moment slips into the past
Leaving us with feeling of regret
Even through our lives are not over yet
For nothing in this world is set
For there will be changes in our lives on that we can bet

We are born young and we grow old
But everyday love can touch our souls
We know that until our lives come to an end
Love can become to us a burden or a friend
For every day I think about how I want my life to be
How when I open my eyes there is someone that I want to see
Someone with an understanding of how much it can mean
When the one that you love also believe in your dreams

Someone's whose love will never grow old with the passage of time
But will remain true regardless of the problems in their hearts and minds
Whose love is steadfast in the recollections of the past
Then that is the kind of love that I want to forever last
I will be able to treasure every moment in the life that I live
Knowing that it is your love that has changed the way that I feel
Being loved by you every day that I grow old brings such comfort to my soul
For every day that I age I know that there are words written about me on a page

Words telling about our lives as we live upon the earth
And how we have shared our love since the beginning of our births
If I would write about you It would be that you were there when I needed you
That you were there to comfort me regardless of what you were going though
Your love touched my heart and left me with a feeling that will never depart
Though I may wish for younger days I know that time has already slipped away

I pray that I am able to leave a love that you can always dream of
For the love that we leave behind is passed along with the passage of time

For with each new generation our love is passed down
As people gather around the tables and sit down
Through the songs that we were able to sing
There is so much love and happiness to each other we are able to bring
Through the words of love written down for all to see
There will not be a dry eye that anyone could see
For the spirit of our love was there for all to see
That showed everyone the way that love could truly come to be

Although I may have wished for younger days
I can see that age has allowed me to pass along my love in a very special way
For as time has passed me by I finally can understand the reasons why
I was meant to be here at this moment and place
For my love to be passed along through time and space
My love lives on in people's hearts to be passed along before they depart
Whether we are young or we are old love will always touch our souls

There Is A Light That I See

There is a light that I can see
I wish that you were here with me
A light so wonderful and bright
Just like the dawning of twilight
There is peace forming inside of me
I wish that you were able to see
So that you would be able to feel
There can be peace in the life that you live

For when I sometimes think of you
I can understand what you are going through
I try to keep a smile upon my face
So that you may feel a love that you can embrace
For when I think about the life that you live
I can truly understand the way that you feel
For when I am looking into your eyes
It is myself that I am able to recognize

For with the love that is deep within our souls
We are joined through a love that was foretold
For with every breath that we take
We know that the love that lives in our heart we can never forsake
Although the world may sometimes blind us to what we can see
We are able to remove the blinders from the eyes of you and me
We are able to search within ourselves and see
There is a light so bright that can reach out and touch the hearts of you and me

For although there will always be problems in the lives that we live
There will always be a love that can help our hearts to heal
For when we are able to hold on to the love that each other give
We are able to change the lives that each other live
Everyday there can be a light that we are able to see
Reaching from the inside of you and me
For as we look upon each other's faces
We can see the light of love that will always leave its traces

Sometimes people close their hearts to what they are able to feel
With no understanding of the loves that they are still able to give
I pray that there is a light that they may one day see

*Coming from deep inside the hearts of you and me
I pray that there will be a light that they may one day see
That will open their eyes to accept what will be their destiny
For when their eyes are open there will be so many memories
Of seeing the love that is being shared by you and me*

*They will know that they can never truly be alone
When in our hearts love has found a home
They will know that for each other they can always care
As they reach out to each other with the love they share
There is a light that I see that reaches into the hearts of you and me
A light that we share with the ones that we care
A light that gives meaning to the lives that we live
Will forever change our lives and the way that we feel*

I Can See The Emotions Behind Your Eyes

I can see the emotions behind your eyes
Emotions that you always seem to try and hide
Yet your feeling are as clear as day
Regardless of the words that I hear you say
For you talk about love without the feelings of your heart
Thinking that I cannot see the truth from the start
Yet for the pleasure of loving you
I blinded myself to knowledge of the truth

For I wanted to believe in you from the start
That you loved me from deep within your heart
But it was me who was denying the truth
That your love for me was never true
I wanted to believe in the innocence of love
For that is what I have always dreamed of
To be with someone whose love that I knew were mine
Those were the thoughts that was often flowing through my mind

To see such love written upon your face
That is what I truly was longing to embrace
I can see the emotions behind your eyes
That can bring out the painful memories that I recognize
For when your love is for someone else
Then I know that you are only thinking of yourself
You are not thinking of the relationship that exists between us
You are not thinking on how to strengthen a love that we can trust

Painful memories of past loves in our lives
Will always make it difficult for a new love to survive
It is time for a change in the way that you feel
It is time for a change in the love that you give
For our lives cannot continue this way
When we are not feeling the love that we need to feel everyday
I can see the emotions behind your eyes
It is time for you to choose if our love will continue to survive

If I Could Catch A Angel In Flight

*If I could catch an Angel in flight
I know that would be such a wonderful sight
For when I looked up into the sky
There would be a tear that fell from my eye
I thought I saw an Angel in flight
An Angel bathed in God's pure light
With the Angel's wings spread out wide
The beauty of the Angel the light could never hide*

*There were so much happiness within my heart
I wanted it to last forever and never depart
Reaching deep into my heart and my soul
I watched as God's love did unfold
I was mesmerized with the beauty that I were able to see
I knew that everyone would have loved to trade places with me
To be where I was at this moment in time
Would live forever in anyone's hearts and minds*

*For to be so blessed with such a sight
Showed me how God's love can forever take flight
How each of us is born into this world
With a love that is worth more than any diamond or pearl
To be blessed with such a sight
To have our hearts filled with sheer delight
We are the children of the light
Nourished and love as we are bathed in God's pure light*

*If I could catch an Angel in flight
I know that would be such a wonderful sight
For when I looked up into the sky
There would be a tear that fell from my eye
For even if there will come the pain of sorrow
I can believe that there will be a better tomorrow
For my heart has been open to truly feel
The love that God gives me in the life that I live*

When Emotions Run Wild

When emotions run wild
The only thing that is left for us to do is smile
For the feelings that we sometimes hold inside
Threatens to rush away from us like the flowing tide
For our memories flow inside of us
Forever changing what we sometimes trust
Affecting everything that we want to do
Even our hopes and our dreams that we want to come true

For when it comes to the things the people do to us
In our hearts there are memories created in us
Memories that we often keep deep inside
Affecting the things that we later decide
Memories of us being treated so wrong
Will live in our hearts for so very long
Slowly changing the way that we feel
Slowly affecting the love that we give

Our lives will always change when we are treated wrong
For we have to find a way to keep our hearts strong
Even if that means blinding ourselves to the truth
We have to find a way to accept what people do
For sometimes when we sleep our minds are wide awake
Struggling with the decisions that we have to make
We are willing to sometimes put aside our pride
To be able to live with the ones that we love by our side

For when the love that we give to is not enough for them to live
They will seek out someone else's love to feel
With no understanding of the pain that it gives
With no understanding of the way that we truly feel
The trust that we give to them is sometimes thrown to the wind
For against us they commit the ultimate sin
The betrayer of a love that has always been true
A love that was given by me and by you

The rising emotions from the memories in our hearts
Sometimes threaten to tear our lives apart
Memories that we keep inside for so many years

Comes back to remind us as we sometimes break down in tears
Yet we have no choice but to reconcile the way we feel
For we still have our lives to live regardless of the way we feel
With the love in our hearts we still have the strength to forgive
Although our hearts may not be able to completely heal

We constantly searching to feel happiness in the lives that we live
When our emotions run wild the only thing that is left for us to do is smile
We can still cry our tears after so many years
Waiting for the feelings of our hearts to completely heal
When our hearts are unable to completely heal
We just have to reconcile the way that we still feel
When living our lives with our hopes and our dreams
When our emotions run wild we can still choose what our lives will mean

Although The Waters May Sometimes Seem Cold

Although the waters may sometimes seem cold
We will continue to wade through them every day that we grow old
For not even the coldness of life will change the way that we feel
When we know that the love in our hearts will help us to heal.
For even as the waters of life will change along the way
We know that we will continue to reach out to each other everyday
Flowing in one direction and then the next
We are left with the decisions that are made simple instead of complex

It is like the thoughts that are going through our minds
Keeps causing us to change over the passage of time
It is like we are destined to reach out to each other
To find a way to reconcile with one another
It is like we are adrift in the water's flow
Praying that we will be taken to where we want to go
It is like the currents are so strong that we are continually being pushed along
Praying that the directions that we are being taken will lead us back home

It is like we are changing courses in mid-stride
Caught up in the times when we have to swim against the tide
It is like the tide can be too strong leaving us with a feeling of being alone
We can wonder if we made the right choice of speaking out with one voice
For when we hold back the words we say a choice was made along the way
We can change the waters that flow with what we come to know
We can turn back the flow of time when we express what is on our minds
For we open people's eyes to see how the waters of life affects you and me

With our thoughts apart of the water's flow from each other we learn and grow
We can teach each other what we need to know we can change the water's flow
For when we are able to work together we will not feel alone in stormy weather
When the waters seem cold we can come together and warm each other's souls
For as the waters continue to flow so will our knowledge continue to grow
For we are all apart of one another we are mothers, fathers, sisters and brothers
For the love in our hearts will always be the bridge that connects us to each other
For the love in our hearts is what we should always share with one another

I Know How You Feel In The Life That You Live

I know how you feel in the life that you live
You see I have been there before with the way I did feel
I know what it means to be afraid to walk through another door
For there were times when I thought I could not go any further
For I have lived the life that I had to live
That is why I know the way that you may sometimes feel
You don't have to be ashamed to cry your tears
For the life that you had to live through the years

You need to let the pain that you feel out
Just go out into the street and shout
Release your fears with your tears
For ahead of you are better years
Release your doubts as to what your life is about
Just go out in the street and shout
Although people may think that you are a little bit crazy
At least the thoughts in your mind will no longer be hazy

You will see what I see that you can change your destiny
You don't have to accept what people may say about you
For when it comes to your life you can make your dreams come true
You See I was once just like you filled with fears and doubts
But after I went out to the street to shout I knew that everything would work out People may have thought that I was a little crazy but my mind was no longer hazy   When we let our fears and doubts out we begin to see what our lives can be about
For we are like a bird that has been set free to truly fulfill our destiny

I know how you feel in the life that you live
You see I have been there before with the way I did feel
I know what it means to be afraid to walk through another door
For there were times when I thought I could not go any further
For I have lived the life that I had to live
That is why I know the way that you may sometimes feel
You don't have to be ashamed to cry your tears
For you have never truly been alone in the life that you had to live

As I Am Sitting And Thinking About The Life That I Live

As I am sitting and thinking about the life that I live
In a moment of desperation I cry my tears
But with a sudden feeling that someone will hear
I tell myself to stop crying before someone will appear
But how can I stop the falling rain
When I need to cry my tears to ease my pain
Given the way that I feel inside from the world I can no longer hide
Even when it goes against my pride I have to release the tears from deep inside

For when my emotions will run deep
It is always hard for me to drift off to sleep
It is hard for me to explain to someone the way I feel
When I don't understand the life that I live
It is hard for me to express my feelings and burdens to another
When there is no communication with my mother, father, sister or brother
I try to do the best that I can to stand up as a woman or man
For I also want to feel pride as I walk among the land

But sometimes in a moment of desperation
My tears will begin to fall without hesitation
Yet I am slowly coming to understand
That our lives do not always go as planned
That I have to learn to accept what I see
And somehow find the strength inside of me
Time has passed by and still there are moments of desperation
When I still cry my tears without any hesitation

But the moments are becoming rare
For I am finally able to be with someone that care
For I am finally able to share the way that I feel
And I can feel an easing of my burdens every day that I live
For I am finally able to believe in my dreams
And understand what my tears sometimes mean
As I am sitting and thinking about the life that I live
I am so grateful that I can talk to someone about the way I feel

Wait And See If Life Will Be Good To You And Me

Wait and see if life will be good to you and me
If we will stay together or set each other free
Wait and see what will come to be
If love will be good to you and to me
For there are times when life can bring two people together
Willing to take a chance that love can last forever
Willing to let love reach into the deeper parts of their hearts
So that a bridge will always exist even after they depart

There is nothing in life that can separate them from one another
When they have given so much of their love to each other
Even when there are times when they have to struggle to live
They will not close their hearts to the love they can feel
For there is nothing more important in the lives that they live
Than to share the love that can help each other's hearts to heal
Wait and see if life will be good to you and to me
If we will stay together or set each other free

Our love can be as strong as another
When we accept that we were meant to be with each other
Our love can be wider than the sea
As we look upon the reflections of you and me
For when our love does not come from deep within
Situations in our lives can bring our love to an end
Through hard times and the problems in our minds
The love in our hearts is what we must continue to find

Wait and see if life will be good to you and to me
If we will stay together or set each other free
Wait and see what will come to be
If our being together was always meant to be
For there are times when life can bring two people together
That are willing to take a chance that love can last forever
That are willing to let love reach into the deeper parts of their hearts
So that a bridge will always exist even after they depart

To Go From A Feeling Of Sadness To Being Able To Smile

To go from a feeling of sadness to being able to smile
Life can be so funny so wonderful and wild
Going from the tears that we may feel to cry
To the dreams that makes us believe we can fly
We are able to change the way that we feel
When we are given a reason to live
Knowing that there are so many people like you and me
We can be amazed at what we sometimes see

With every sound that we hear rather it is coming from far or near
There are the memories within our minds that appear and disappear
There are the memories that we continue to let go
As the feelings within our hearts continue to grow
Our feelings can change from fear to love and love to fear
As we try and understand everything that we hear
Fear and love, love and fear as we walk across the land
Our thoughts drifting around like the blowing of the sand

With our eyes there are so many things that we see
As we search to define what we want our lives to be
Within our hearts we change the way that we feel
For there is always someone seeking the love we can give
For when the love that we see brings us happiness and joy
We can recall the memories of being a girl or a boy
We can always find a way to turn our sadness into a smile
Like the currents in the ocean our lives can be filled with so much emotion

To go from a feeling of sadness to being able to smile
Life can be so funny so wonderful and wild
Going from the tears that we may feel to cry
To the dreams that makes us believe we can fly
We are able to change the way that we feel
When we are given a reason to live
Knowing that there are so many people like you and me
We can be amazed at what we sometimes see

Let Us Not Sleep The Day Away

*Let us not sleep the day away
When there are so many words that we need to say
To let someone know that we are there
Just waiting to give them our love and care
Letting them know that the love in our hearts will never disappear
Even when the words that they say may not be what we want to hear
Let us not sleep the day away and regret the words that we never say
For each moment can be precious and rare as we give each other love and care*

*Although there are changes in the lives that we live
The love that we share we should be always be willing to give
For we know the meaning of the love that we share
When people come to us from everywhere
For they are waiting for a chance to feel
A love reaching out to them that is wonderful and real
Given our own pain and our sacrifice
We can understand that feeling love is worth any price*

*We can understand how someone will feel
If they are not receiving the love that they need to live
We came to understand that the love that we give
Has the power to change the lives that we live
For we know how our hearts may be tender and easy to break
When the love that we give people forsake
Never understanding that they are leading us down a road
When the love in our hearts can sometimes turn cold*

*Turning our hearts around as we go falling to the ground
We can reach out our hands praying that someone will be around
Even as our tears settle into the dust we find it hard to give someone else our trust Yet slowly we begin to regain our confidence as our lives start to make sense.
For as we place ourselves in each other's shoes
We begin to understand how precious are the moments we lose
Let us not sleep the day away when there are so many words we need to say
There are so many people waiting for us to share our love when we pass their way*

When We Are Looking Through The Mirror What Do We See

When we are looking through the mirror what do we see
Will we see a reflection that reflects what is in the hearts of you and me
Calling back to us that in ourselves we need to have trust
Even when there are situations that seems to get the best of us
For through life's ups and downs
There will be changes and turnarounds
Looking through the mirror will we be able to see traces
From an inner strength left in so many places

For in our hearts there is a courage that we can feel
A courage that can keep us strong in the lives that we live
Can there be any wonder if there are tears that comes to our eyes
For looking at ourselves there is nothing that we can hide.
Looking through the mirror and seeing our faces
Gives us an understanding that our lives leaves it's traces
For there comes a time when we all need to face the truth
That the world is in need of the love coming from me and you

It seems like every day that goes by their are children with tears in their eyes
Looking around for someone to wipe their tears dry and to explain the reasons why
Everyday someone is in need of encouragement that can help them to succeed
Looking into the mirror we can be the ones to give them the love they need
We should not close our eyes to what we see for that could one day be you and me
For sometimes there is only you and me that can help to change their destiny
We should not close our hearts to what we feel and continue with the lives we live
When there are people waiting for the love that we are able to give

When we look into the mirror we can see the traces of a love
A love that exists for the ones that we think of
Looking into the mirror coming from you and me
There is a inner strength that we are able to see
Through life's turnarounds and ups and downs
In our hearts there will always be a inner strength to be found
Looking into the mirror there is a reflection of you and me
With thoughts of love for the people that we

When Imagination Is Lost

When our imaginations are lost
We will be the ones to pay the cost
For there are places that we will never see
Without the imagination in you and me
For the beginning of our dreams coming true
Comes from the ideas within the hearts of me and you
For when we let our imagination soar
We find that we can hold the key to every door

With a door to the world of make believe
We are able to create a future that we can perceive
We are able to change what happens over time
Which gives us a fulfillment within our hearts and minds
For when our imaginations are able to flow
There is so much knowledge that we come to know
Within our imaginations there can be no lie
For our imaginations will live until the day we die

Through the lives of every generation
There are minds with such illumination
That they bring out such a spark of creation
That it reaches into our souls to ignite our own imaginations
Without our imaginations where would we be
We would be just an empty shell that everyone would see
With no hope of our dreams ever coming true
There can be no inspiration in the hearts of me and you

For we need our imaginations to help keep us alive
For they nourish our dreams which helps us to survive
When our imaginations are lost
We are not the only ones that will pay the cost
For our eyes will never be open to see
The Fulfillment of our true destinies
To light the way for the people who pray
That our imaginations can change the world some day

Changing Values Can Sometimes Set What Is Wrong Right

Changing values can sometimes set what's wrong right
Changing values can sometimes set our hearts in flight
Changing values can change our lives whether it is day or night
Bringing back into our lives the wonder of God's light
For many times we can see our lives in a different light
Turning a place that once was dark very bright
Changing values can change our lives in mid-flight
Opening our eyes once again to such a heavenly sight

For when we tell ourselves that our lives can have so much meaning
We are reminding our hearts of the dreams that makes our lives worth living
We are dreaming the dreams that can change our lives from the start
The dreams that can bring back a feeling of love that is so precious to our hearts
With the changing values we are opening our eyes to see
That there is a light that has always been inside the hearts of you and me
When our lives seem dark we cannot look deep inside our hearts
We cannot see the love that can ignite a brightness hidden from the start

We can look into a mirror and see a reflection of who we are
We can see within our hearts the rising of a star
For the sharing of our love is always worth the price
When it comes to the sharing of our love we should never think twice
When we see that changing values can sometimes set what's wrong right
We can see that changing values can sometimes set our hearts in flight
Bringing back the love that we are able to feel
We can see that changing values changes the lives that we will live

When we are letting people control the lives that we live
We know that one day there may be regrets in the way that we feel
Changing values and the changing of our lives
Some times that is what we need to keep our hopes and dreams alive
We can look into the mirror and see a reflection of you and me
We can remember the persons that we used to be
For when we are changing our values we are changing our lives
We are discovering the meaning behind our struggles to stay alive

A Quiet Place For Me To Be

There is a quiet place for me to be
Where I can feel an easing of the burdens inside of me
A place where I can feel my heart live again
A place where I am able to accept my sins
A place where I can reflect upon the road that I have taken
To understand what it means when the feelings deep inside has been awaken
There is a quiet place for me to be
Where I can find that peace inside of me

For who can say what will happen tomorrow
Whether it will be a time of happiness or sorrow
For who can say if we will still be alive
When it comes to the situations in which we struggle to survive
When we think about all of the people that we meet
We do not know if one day they will be living in the streets
For who can say what will happen tomorrow
If their hearts will be filled with happiness or sorrow

Do you not think that they are also searching for a quiet place
Even if it will be in such a tiny space
For what value can be placed on that feeling of peace
When in the heart and mind all life's struggles have ceased
We should not be afraid to look them in the eyes
To let them know to not be afraid of the secrets they try to hide
For there will be a quiet place for them to open their eyes and see
That they do not have to be afraid of what will come to be

For as we come into this world either as a boy or a girl
Within each of our hearts there is a diamond and pearl
Fashioned from the love that lives in our hearts
For that is what we search to feel from the start
When we close our eyes we can be in that quiet place
A place where time has so much meaning in the hearts of every race
For even a moment can seem to last forever
For when the heart is at peace all moments can come together

I Am In The Eye Of A Storm

I am in the eye of a storm and I am safe from any harm
For there is a calmness that I am able to feel in the midst of my struggles to live
There are the flashing of lights and the sudden downpours
There are crackling sounds from the hinges on the doors
In the eye of the storm is where I stand even when my life does not go as planned
Even when there is so much destruction as I look out across the land
For I know that I have did the best that I could as a man
Reaching out my hand trying to help the people around me stand

I cannot remember ever feeling this way
For I feel better than any other day
Perhaps it is the thought of where I would be
If I had not opened my eyes to truly see
That I have to be the one to take control of my destiny
For regardless of what other people tell me that they see
They still cannot look on the inside of me
To see the love in my heart that came to be

I can look out at the world in my own way
Regardless of what other people will do or say
For they cannot look on the inside of me
And determine what they want my life to be
For no matter what they learn in the lives they live
They will never be able to tell me the way that I feel
For each of us must walk in our own shoes
That is what each of us has the freedom to choose

For we can choose to allow ourselves to burn with fire
Where there will be no peace in our hearts even after we retire
There will be no rest from the constant struggles that put our lives to the test
When we cannot accept in our hearts that we did our best
I am in the eye of a storm and I am safe from any harm
For there is a calmness that I am able to feel in the midst of my struggles to live
For I know that I was able to share a love that helped other people to heal
For there is nothing more precious in life than the love that we are able to give

It Is Not Your Burden To Bear

It is not your burden to bear even for the ones that you truly care
For they are blessed just to have you there
For within their hearts they are able to feel your love and care
And they know that the love that you give is truly rare
To be a child with so much love for your father and mother
To be a child with so much love for your sisters and brothers
It is not your burden to bear even for the ones that you truly care
For they are receiving a blessing just to have you there

When you see the way that they are being treated everyday
You may wonder why they are being treated that way
For there are so many things that you have yet to realize
Such as the heartaches that can be felt in our struggle to survive
You may sometimes see a smiling face and the tears that you can trace
You may feel that sudden need to give them a loving embrace
To remind them that in the lives that they live
You will always be willing to give them the love that they can feel

You may bear a burden for the tears in their eyes
For the way that you feel can sometimes be hard to describe
For there can be tears in your heart that can only slowly depart
When you see the ones that you love begin to heal from the start
For you wish that you could take their pain away
With the love that you are willing to give everyday
It is not your burden to bear
Even though there are things that happen to them that you are aware

You cannot change the actions that they will take
For they may not understand the choices that they make
You cannot take responsibility for what someone will do along the road they take
For they must take responsibility for the choices that they make
When all of your advice falls on deaf ears you cannot bear their tears
For their tears are for them to bear regardless of how much you truly care
Although they may stumble and fall along the road that they take
In the living of their lives it is still their decisions to make
You cannot cover them with your wings
And try to take responsibility for everything
You need to let them live their lives the best that they can
Even when in your heart you may not truly understand

Love and pain anger and jealousies affect the ones that we love everyday
For them to reconcile the feelings within their hearts we can only pray
When they do not listen to what we have to say
We need to give them the space to live their lives in their own way

You need to reconcile the way that you feel
You need to move on with the life that you live
You do not need to worry about what anyone will say
You need to treasure the moments that life gives you everyday
Allow God to heal your heart with the love that he gives
Give your burdens to God and allow your heart to heal
It is not your burden to bear even for the ones that you truly care
For them it will always be a blessing you are willing to give them love and care

Every Day I Want You To Open Your Eyes To See

Every day I want you to open your eyes to see
That there will always be a love that will exist between you and me
Every day I want you to open your eyes to see
That there was a reason that life brought you to me
For you needed someone whose love would always be true
Someone who was willing to understand what life could put you through
For you were in search of someone who would always be there
Willing to always give you their love and care

Someone who will be there when your heart is burning with fire
Someone that would try to give you what you truly desire
Someone who will not turn away when you showed them anger
But who would stay with you even in times of danger
There may be times when you feel you face too much sacrifice
There are times when I will be there to give you advice
It will be your choice to think about it twice
To understand the love that I give to you is beyond price
I want you to open your eyes and think about what you would be going through
If I turned around and no longer gave my love to you
I wonder if you could feel a joy in your heart
If from your life I would truly depart
I am letting you know the way that I truly feel
So that you may understand what matters the most in the life you live
Every day I want you to open your eyes to see
That there will always be a love that will exist between you and me

When you close your eyes you may be able to imagine this
That I am the one person in your life that you would truly miss
That there would be an absence of the love that you needed to live
A love that you would always be seeking to feel
When you close your eyes you do not have to imagine this
For as I hold you close you can still feel my kiss
Every day I want you to open your eyes to see
That there will always be a love that will exist between you and me

Our Wit's End

When we are at our wit's end
It is a time when we can no longer pretend
For our eyes have been open to see
It is time that we accept the changes in you and me
For when we look at a picture of yesterday
We can see that time has slipped away
We can see the youthful way that we used to look
In the pictures that are hanging on the hooks

We can open our photo albums and see
The pictures that is so precious to you and me
For they bring back the memories of you and me
When our lives was as wonderful as can be
Surely there have been some regrets
But the lives that we are living are not over yet
There have been the moments when tears were in our eyes
But that could have come from the love we realized

From the moments when we saw each other
We knew that we wanted to be with one another
The moments of meeting each other's fathers and mothers
Made us happy that we had met one another
For there was a love that was flowing through
That reached into the hearts of me and you
Praying that we could continue to take our relationship much further
We knew that in our hearts we could be good fathers and mothers

When we are old and sometimes feeling cold
We will still love each other deep down in our souls
When we are sitting down and looking at yearbooks
We will look back down the road that we took
There were many directions that we could have taken
That could have caused our love for each other to be forsaken
When we feel that we are at our wit's end we don't have to pretend
For we know that our love for one another will never end

A Message For The Ones That We Love

When I have lived my life for so long
When I have seen things that were right and wrong
There is only one place where I will truly belong
The place where God has prepared for me when he calls me home
When I walked along the river's edge
In my heart I will truly pledge
That I will allow the love in my heart
To bring people together that were separated from the start

For I will show love to the people that I meet
Even when there are times when we will compete
When I have lived my life for so long I want to be able to feel
That I have truly changed the lives that people had to live
Although I cannot be in some places
The places where I go I want to leave traces
I want to see the smiles written across people's faces
That tells me of a love that always leaves its traces

When I have lived my life for so long I want to always remember
That I was not afraid to share my love from the month of January to December
That I was not afraid of what people would say or do
When I showed them that the love in my heart was true
When I have lived my life for so long
When I have lived my life in a one room shack home
I have learned that beauty is in the eye of the beholder
For the beauty that we see changes as we grow older

When I have lived my life for so long
When I have seen things that was right and wrong
There is only one place where I will truly belong
The place where God has prepared for me when he calls me home
When I have walked along the river's edge
In my heart I will truly pledge
That I will allow the love in my heart
To bring people together that was separated from the start

I Am Closing My Eyes To Sleep

It seems like I am closing my eyes to sleep
For there are old friends that I seek to meet
For there is nothing that I want more
Than to walk with them along the distant shore
For there are so many matters that we can talk about
For with each other we never had to scream and shout
For with every word that we are able to hear
It brings the sound of love to our ears

I am light of feet as we walk along the lighted street
For it seems like the street and the sandy shores often come together to meet
It is always so fascinating for me to see
The way that our love for each other can come to be
In me there is no feeling of pain
Even in the burning heat or in the pouring rain
It is as if the weather has no power of me
It just brings out the beauty that I am able to see

Such moments like this is ever so precious to me
To be able to wonder what I can truly be
To be able to meet with old friends again
Fills my heart with a love that I never want to end
Everything is again changing before my eyes
Bringing me back to the place that I barely recognize
I have to let go of my visions of the distant shore
Until the moments come again when I can be there once more

To meet with my family and my friends
In a day of homecoming that will never end
There is such a feeling of love within my heart
A love that I never want to depart
Everything is changing before my eyes
But there will always be a love that I am able to recognize
It seems like I am closing my eyes to sleep
For there are old friends that I have been waiting to me

I Often Wonder If I Will Awaken In The Morning Light

I often wonder if I will awake in the morning light
Or will I pass away in the dark of the night
I often wonder when my life will come to an end
If I will be forgiven for my sins
For I am still able to remember some of the things I did in the past
I still have regrets for the moments that I let pass
For there were words that I did not say
When someone that loved me came my way

There were times when my eyes were not open to see
That so many people came to truly care about me
For my heart was not open to feel
The love that some people were willing to give
I should have taken the time and allowed people
To share the love in their hearts and minds
I have not released my soul yet
My heart is filled with so much regret

Until my soul is released I may not know the true meaning of peace
For I will not know if my sins are forgiven until I depart the world of the living
As I await the ending of my life I will bear the pain and sacrifice
For I can no longer pretend that it is not hard to bear the weight of my sins
I can only ask that you pray for this lost soul whose heart was once cold
For I now cry my tears for the ones that I pained through the years
From listening to the words from the Bible
For my actions I know that I have always been libel

I have learned so much coming to the end of my life
I have heard the words from the bible regarding love pain and sacrifice
I have heard the words of forgiveness for which I am truly in need
I pray that in my quest for forgiveness I can succeed
As I await the end of my life, I will bear the pain and sacrifice
For the actions that were taken I should have thought about twice
Until my soul is released, I may not know the true meaning of peace
For I will not know if my sins are forgiven until I depart the world of the living

Seeing Myself Everyday

*Seeing myself everyday makes me want to kneel down and pray
That I will be at peace when my soul is finally released
For listening to the words that people say leaves a love I can feel everyday
For the life that I have lived and the pain that I caused other people to feel
I have the deepest regret for the things that I did in the life I had to live
For I was unable to see the truth of what I was putting other people through
When they were there to try and help me with the things that I had to do
There were many words that I did say that pushed people away from me everyday*

*I find myself returning to that time with such thoughts flowing through my mind
That I want to kneel down and pray for having pushed people away
With so much time passing me by I know the day is coming when I will die
Within my heart I can no longer lie as I express my feelings with the tears I cry
Today I must face the truth of what I have put other people through
For I know that I will never be at peace until my soul is finally released
Listening to the words that people say leaves me with a feeling of love everyday
For their were words of forgiveness is expressed through their love everyday*

*Seeing such devotion and strength of character in the people that I see
Causes me to re-evaluate the feelings deep inside of me
Causes me to change my perspective in life
Even my feelings of pain and sacrifice
I can finally come to understand the lives we sometimes have to live
And why we are always given a reason to forgive
For everything in life carries its own price
Whether we are being mean or whether we are being nice*

*Fade to black fade to white fade to the light fade to the night
Which choice do we make to help us sleep peacefully in the night
I find myself returning to that time with such thoughts flowing through my mind*

*That I want to kneel down and pray for having pushed people away
With so much time passing me by I know the day is coming when I will die
Within my heart I can no longer lie as I express my feelings with the tears I cry
Fade to black fade to white fade to the light fade to the night
We must all decide within our hearts to do what we know is right*

The Time We Let Pass Us By

How the time has passed by leaving me with a feeling to cry
For there has been so many people that I have told hello and good-bye
People that have come into my life and made me laugh and made me cry
That gave me the dreams that will live in my heart even after I will die
How the moments have slipped away to leave me reaching out for them everyday
To reach for the good times that poured love into my heart and mind
How the moments have slipped away leaving me to reach out for what used to be
The moments of happiness of being with family and friends

For I am still here as I live my life year by year
Knowing that at any moment from the world I could disappear
Mixed with the love that grows inside of me
There is a feeling of pain that resides in me
There will be a feeling of regret in my heart
For allowing a separation to exist with the ones that love me from the start
For not taking the time to slow down the life that I live
I missed out on the love that some people were willing to give
It is not something that we think about beforehand
It is something later on in life we come to understand
That we should have taken the time in the lives that we live
We should have treasured the moments that made our lives so wonderful to live
For our lives should not be measured by the money that we can earn
But by the time that we spend with one another expressing our love and concern
It is not too late if we no longer continue to hesitate
For we can still create the moments of happiness along the road that we take

How the time has passed by leaving me with a feeling to cry
For there has been so many people that I have told hello and good-bye
People that have come into my life and made me laugh and made me cry
That gave me the dreams that will live in my heart even after I will die
Each moment that is given to us is a blessing in the lives that we live
For we are being given a chance to see our dreams fulfilled
It is something that we think about over the passage of time
That love should always be given from our hearts and minds

The Memories Of Your Love Live On In Me

Time has passed that I can see for I am not the way that I used to be
For I used to wonder when I was young what would be my destiny
For the winter's cold reaches beneath my clothes
Making to wonder about the life that I have chose
For I am now shivering from the cold drops of rain
That leaves me with a feeling of awkwardness instead of pain
For every raindrop that falls seems to be calling my name.
Is this truly the life that you want to claim?

Although I am shivering from the cold
I can feel a peace deep within my soul
A peace coming from the memories of the past
Bringing out a smile in me at last
A smile that is so bright that even in the freezing night
It has taken away my feelings of fright
For I am able to stop shivering in the freezing cold
For there is so much love that I can feel deep within my soul

Time has passed that I can see bringing back the memories of you and me
A time when we held each other close and felt the love that we needed the most
That feeling of comfort and safety being held in each other's arms
Gave us a feeling that we would always keep each other safe from harm
For even with the raindrops falling down there was laughter in me to be found
Time has passed that I can see but still the memories of your love lives in me
If I was given the choice to turn back the hands of time
I would turn it back to the moments when I felt your hands in mine

Time has passed that I can see for I am not the way that I used to be
For I used to wonder when I was young what would be my destiny
For the winter's cold reaches beneath my clothes
Making to wonder about the life that I have chose
Time has passed that I can see but still the memories of your love lives in me
I truly realized how precious each moment became with you a part of my destiny
If I was given the choice to turn back the hands of time
I would turn it back to the moments when I felt your heart beating next to mine

About The Author

Poetry is something that we all share, each time that we think a thought. We think in poetry, only some of us are not able to put it in words but thoughts of poetry live in our hearts. We are filled with emotions and that is what poetry is. You need to just open your heart to the words written for they are the words coming from a heart just like you. From our pain and our sacrifices to our joy and happiness, when you read this, we will be able to see that we are all the same seeking love and a dream that we can claim.

There are times when we may feel lost and there is nothing that we can do. The truth is that there will always be options for us to choose. Only with our ever-changing emotions at the time we are blind to see. For every action there is an opposite reaction. There are things that we know that we can do yet we get caught up in the things that we are going through. There are times when we are happy and times when we are sad. It is a delicate balance in the lives that we live. Each of us will need to come to grips with the way that we feel. We are never alone although we think at the time that we are alone. We need to find the courage to reach out and say that we are here. Is there anyone out there that cares about the lives that we live? At the end of the day if we listen closely, we will be able to hear a voice saying that I am here, you are not alone. Ever changing emotions are what will live in our hearts. We just have to decide the things that we want to do and find the courage to follow them through.

The life that I have had to live has been very difficult but the love in my heart kept me strong even when I sometimes may have felt alone. I have cried my share of tears and I have suffered for many years but I have kept the love in my heart. We are human and we make mistakes but as long as we live there will always be another road for us to take.

I pray that the poems that you are reading help you to understand that we all go through life's ever-changing emotions. We have to live in the moment and if that moment continues to last then we should remember that our lives are made up of our past, present and our future. For as long as we live, we can change the way that we feel. Love and forgiveness is what we should always hold most precious in our lives. Love and forgiveness can forever live in our hearts. Poetry is something that we all share, each time that we think

a thought. We think in poetry, only some of us are not able to put it in words but thoughts of poetry live in our hearts. We are filled with emotions and that is what poetry is. You need to just open your heart to the words written for they are the words coming from a heart just like you. From our pain and our sacrifices to our joy and happiness, when you read this, we will be able to see that we are all the same seeking love and a dream that we can claim.
Within our lives we feel happiness, sorrow and pain, sometimes even all at once.

There are many times when we do not understand the way that we feel. There are times when we want to strengthen the relationships in the lives that we live but pride is what we still feel. Sometimes we are breaking apart even when it is very painful in our hearts.
Sometimes we would rather live with misery than reconcile with the ones that we love.

There will always be mistakes made in the lives that we live. We need to work past the problems in our lives to find a solution. I know that we can still feel hurt but we can overcome that feeling when we look deeply into our hearts. There will always be a love that we will feel for the ones that we love. Accepting this is the one true constant that can strengthen our relationships. I hope that with the reading of this poetry you will be given an insight. We do not live in a perfect world, but we are a diamond or a pearl.

We are all special in our own ways. We all deserve to be loved every day.

www.ingramcontent.com/pod-product-compliance
Lightning Source LLC
LaVergne TN
LVHW051951060526
838201LV00059B/3596